The Caribbean People

Book 1

Lennox Honychurch

Nelson Caribbean

Thomas Nelson and Sons Ltd
Lincoln Way, Windmill Road, Sunbury-on-Thames, Middlesex, TW16 7HP
P.O. Box 73146, Nairobi, Kenya
95 Church Street, P.O. Box 943, Kingston, Jamaica
308–312 Lockhart Road Golden Coronation Bldg 2/F Blk A Hong Kong
116-D JTC Factory Office Bldg Lorong 3, Geylarg Square, Singapore 14

Thomas Nelson (Australia) Ltd
19–39 Jeffcott Street, West Melbourne, Victoria 3003

Thomas Nelson and Sons (Canada) Ltd
81 Curlew Drive, Don Mills, Ontario

Thomas Nelson (Nigeria) Ltd
8 Ilupeju Bypass, PMB 21303, Ikeja, Lagos

Designed by Hedgehog Design
Illustrations by Hedgehog Design and Peter Bailey
Phototypeset by Tradespools Ltd, Frome, Somerset
Printed in Hong Kong

Acknowledgements

I am grateful to a number of people for their assistance during the
writing of this book. I am particularly indebted to Daphne Agar and
Mary Narodny of Morne Rouge, Dominica, for doing everything
possible towards helping me complete *The Caribbean People*. I also
thank Carol Bunting for her advice and corrections while working on
the manuscript.

Cornelia Henry and her staff at the Roseau Public Library made my
research easier. I must also make mention of the students of the
Young Adults Class 1976 of the Dominica Community High School
who were the 'guinea pig' pupils for much of what appears in this
book.

About this book

We who live on the islands and in the countries of the Caribbean are living in exciting times. Many changes are taking place in our lands, our peoples, and our societies. To learn how to deal with these challenges, we must know how they came about. By learning from the past, we can build for the future. This is why we study history.

This book tells us about the early history of the Caribbean people. As we will find out, history goes back thousands of years. Long before men arrived in the Caribbean from Europe and Africa there were cities, villages, religions and systems of government on the islands and on the mainland of the Americas.

In Part 1 we find out how man first came to the continents of North and South America and to the Caribbean area. We shall learn about the hunters, fishermen, farmers and warriors who roamed the land and sea, and about the great kingdoms which they built in Central and South America, and their settlements on the islands.

In Part 2 we learn what was happening in other parts of the world at that time. For thousands of years the people of Africa, Asia and Europe knew almost nothing of each other. Their societies developed separately from one another, until at last explorers came upon new lands.

People from all parts of the world have settled in the Caribbean area. Races and customs have mixed with one another to create the people and the systems we know today. *The Caribbean People, Book 1* tells us of our early history so that we may understand not only about the people of the region, but also about the land upon which we live.

Lennox Honychurch

Contents

Part One

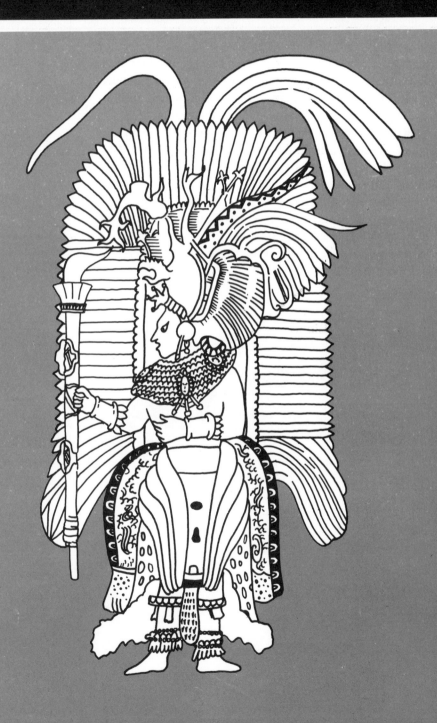

1. Across the continent

We are the people of the Caribbean lands. To the north and south of us lie two large continents where men of every race live and where the climate and landscape vary from icy tundra to large, dry desert. There are mighty rivers and lakes, forests, mountain ranges and wide grassy plains. These continents and all the islands which surround them are known as the 'Americas'. North and South America are separated from other continents of the world by two great oceans: the Atlantic and the Pacific.

When and how did mankind first come to the Americas and the Caribbean? Over the years this has puzzled scientists, but most of them agree that man first came to the Americas by way of Asia. If we look at a map of the world we will see a narrow stretch of water, called the Bering Strait, separating Alaska from the coast of Siberia in north-eastern Asia.

The path of the Mongolians across the 'land-and-ice bridge' of the Bering Strait.

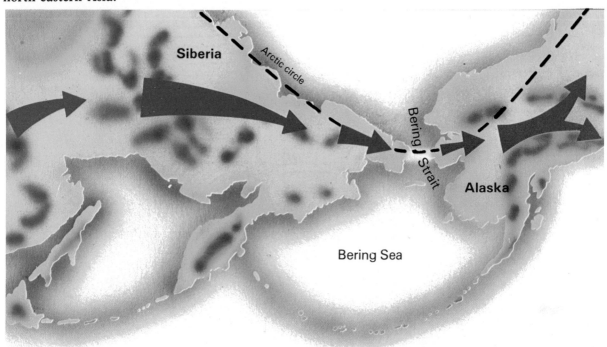

Siberia

Arctic circle

Bering Strait

Alaska

Bering Sea

North Pacific Ocean

The land and the people

Thirty thousand years ago the cold ice-cap of the world spread much further south than the Arctic does today. This cold period, or Ice Age, lasted for thousands of years, after which the ice melted and withdrew once more. The last Ice Age was 10 000 years ago, when men were able to walk across the Bering Strait. Scientists are not agreed on when the first men came to America.

The human race had lived in other continents of the world for thousands of years before they came to America. Rough, short, hairy men roamed across Africa, Europe and Asia, following herds of wild animals which they killed for food. Bare stone caves or the crotches of trees were the only homes and shelter they had, for they did not know how to build. Meat was almost all they had to eat, for they did not know much about food. They collected fruit but did not know how to grow the plants they wanted. To keep warm they wrapped themselves

Hunters followed mammoths and other animals as they moved from one grazing ground to another.

9

in the skins of beasts they slaughtered.

Man learned to chip bits of stone to make them sharp. These points could pierce, scrape and cut, and so he used these stones as tools for killing animals and cleaning skins. He tied the stones to sticks and slowly developed axes and spears in this way. Because no one was able to record the events of these early humans, they are known as 'Prehistoric' men, and the only way we can find out about them is to study the bones and tools which they left behind.

Man was a late-comer to the Americas. In those times men followed the wild beasts for food and some tribes followed wandering herds up the length of Asia and across the land-and-ice bridge at the Bering Strait.

Over a period of hundreds of years various groups came to North America in this way and found themselves in a new land. These people were of the Mongolian race. The people of eastern Asia are Mongolians.

The Ice Age mammals had come east from Siberia into Alaska in search of food in greener pastures. Their wanderings led them further south into the grasslands of North America. The Mongolians followed. They were the first people in an empty land which spread itself eastwards to the Atlantic shores of Canada, southwards across the deserts, through tropical South America and along the Andes range of mountains to the tip of Chile.

The societies which developed across this vast land, beginning with those first Mongolian wanderers, were amazing. There were societies that dwelt in permanent settlements: some were democratic, in which everyone had a say in running the affairs of the tribe; some had very strict class systems, based on property and wealth. Some were ruled by human gods carried about on litters; some had systems of justice, while others punished by torture. There were tribes ruled by warriors and tribes ruled by women, by sacred elders and by councils. There were tribes who worshipped bison or the maize by which they lived. In short, there was a great diversity of Indian nations, speaking over five hundred languages, and it all began with those first Mongolian wanderers.

After 10 000 BC (before the birth of Christ) the ice-cap receded and the Bering Strait became sea once more. The only way people could come to the Americas after that was by boat. The ice moved south and retreated three times and with each retreat the land changed. When the glaciers withdrew to the north for the last time in our history, the climate and plants of North America also changed. The large prehistoric animals could no longer feed the hunters, for the giant hairy mammoths and caribou died out. The wandering men then had to change their ways and three types of livelihood developed.

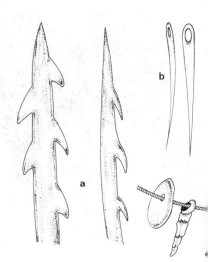

Some tribes continued to hunt and gather the smaller animals and new plants. Other tribes kept to the sea-coast and specialised in sea-food gathering. The third group gathered food from plants and grain

(above) The early Americans lived in caves.

(left) An Amerindian using a blowpipe to hunt.

(below) **a** harpoons, **b** needles, **c** beads, **d** spearheads, **e** fishhooks and **f** gouges made of shell and bone.

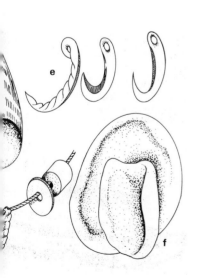

from wild grasses. So the hunters, fishermen and wild vegetation gatherers moved about the two continents, pushing further across their new-found land. We must remember that the time was 8 000 BC, and they wandered for thousands of years. Living together in groups made men want to exchange ideas, and whenever this happens in any society one can expect great changes. And so they slowly improved their tools and ways of life. Besides the forces of nature, they depended on each other for survival.

The hunters

The hunters were the largest of the three groups and adapted to the vast forest-covered stretches of both continents. Here the game was mostly small animals, but in the wide prairie grasslands of North America the hunters followed bison, or buffalo, as they grazed across the plains. As the hunters moved they lived in camps, very often caves, to which they returned each season.

The women of the tribe took care of the children and scraped clean the furry animal hides, among other duties. The men, armed only with stone-tipped spears, circled a bear or bison and hurled their rough weapons at the animal. They dragged the carcase to the shelter, and the tribe gathered round to help flay the skin. Bits of meat were hung over the campfire to roast, but most of it was left to be eaten by animals and birds.

The hides were most valuable. They could be worn as aprons or wraps, or hung in the doorway of the cave. And when they were laid on the floor, the furry softness was a great improvement on the cold stone or damp earth! With their edges tied together hides served as water bags or as carriers for roots and fruits. Much later the hunters, by putting a number of hides over strong poles, made a warm shelter, called a 'tepee', for themselves.

On cold nights the hunters gathered around the warm fires in their caves and told stories about their greatest adventures, and of the lives and brave deeds of men who had lived many years before. To record these stories, the hunters scratched pictures on the walls of the caves. Using red, yellow, and white clay, and black charcoal from the fires, they drew hunting scenes.

In parts of America the hunters developed new tools. They invented the bow and arrow. To work properly, the spear had to be modified into a light and well-balanced arrow. What a change this was for the hunters! No longer did they have to get close to the animals to kill them.

In the tropical forests of the Amazon River Basin, hunters lived in the hot, dense jungles and sheltered in rough huts of sticks and leaves. Besides bows and arrows they developed the blowpipe. This was a long, thin, wooden tube into one end of which was placed an arrow dart; the hunter put the other end to his mouth and gave a sharp, strong blow through the tube. This forced the dart to shoot out. Many birds were caught in this way, and after shooting them the hunters put the colourful feathers in their hair, and through their ears and noses. There was no need for warm animal hides and so they roamed through the forests naked, with perhaps only strips of leaves around their waists for decoration.

The fishermen

As the large mammals which once roamed across America became extinct, hunting became less productive. So many tribes turned to eating the meat of shellfish which were available in large numbers along the Atlantic and Pacific coasts. Today, archaeologists who study the past people of America still come across large piles of shells which were deposited by early fishermen. The fact that food could be gathered along the shores meant that small groups of people could give up their wandering existence.

With time, their knowledge of sea life increased. Catching fish posed a difficult problem, but by trial and error the fish-gatherers developed the line and hook. Lines were made from animal gut and hooks were shaped from shell and bone. They found out that a sharp barb on the end of a hook would catch in the throat of the fish.

They adapted the hunting spear so that it could be used in the sea. This tool was called the harpoon. It was carved from bone and incised with barbs to hold the fish. In the tropical river valleys of South America the hunters used bows and arrows to shoot fish close to the surface of the water. The Arawak and Carib people who settled in the Caribbean used this method of fishing and earlier tribes left piles of shells on the islands. They found the coral reefs full of fish which were easy to catch and collect. These fishing groups all over the American continents made a great variety of tools—knives, chisels, awls, needles, fishhooks, pikes, harpoons and beads.

Present-day Indian canoes on a tributary of the Amazon in South America.

These people on the banks of rivers and seashores wanted to reach other areas along the coast, across the lake or river where they lived. Now came the time when the first rough boat or canoe was built. Over the years of working near the water they realised that tree trunks could support the weight of men. Soon they thought that if they could sit *in* the tree trunk, rather than *on* it, the trunk would remain more steady.

To hollow out a tree trunk with a flint knife was very difficult, but charred wood is much easier to scrape away than green wood. So the fishermen lit fires along the tree trunk and scraped away the charred wood as the fire burnt down. These dugout canoes were much better for travelling.

In other parts of America fishermen and hunters were making canoes in other ways. They made frames of saplings, spread bark or animal skins across them, and tied them fast with cord.

The manner of their fishing.

(left) This picture shows Indians fishing in a dugout canoe. In the distance other fishermen can be seen harpooning fish.

While the men were away hunting, the women and children gathered wild fruits.

The food-gatherers

As the hunters in the cooler regions followed the herds, they came across many seeds and wild fruits which they could pick and eat. These tribes of food-gatherers ranged along western North America down to Central Mexico. In these regions there were annual harvests of acorns, nuts, grass seeds, berries and roots fit to eat. These wild crops had to be collected wherever they grew, and the food-gatherers required containers to store the harvest so they would have some left to eat later. At this time, in about 6 000 BC, these people were making baskets from vines and tree bark.

These basket-makers gathered the vegetables and seeds in the baskets, some of which they stored away in storage pits in floors of caves. One of the advanced customs of these basket-making people was their clothes. The men wore simple loin cloths, and the women

wore apron-skirts. These garments were not made of skins but of cloth, woven from fibres which women had chewed from the tough, sword-like leaves of the yucca plant. Gradually the basket-makers added designs to their work. The rough patterns were probably magic symbols to bring good luck. Some baskets were plastered inside with mud and gum to make them watertight.

The making of baskets was followed after many years by the making of pottery. The knowledge of pottery-making took thousands of years to be developed by American man. The clay plaster on the baskets may have led to the making of pots. Soon it was realised that fire hardened clay. Five thousand years ago the first large bowls and small jars were made by tribes on the coast of Ecuador. These pots were thick and heavy, but decorations were produced by simple instruments, such as pieces of shell, sharpened sticks, or fingers.

Then came the time when some of the food-gatherers changed their way of life. The largest single step in the history of any people is when they change from a nomadic, wandering life to settle in one place. The food-gatherers had depended on the seasons' natural harvest for their supply of food. But there were times of cold or drought which cut down on the supply of wild berries and seeds. By some strange event, American man found that he could make seeds grow and gradually he began to plant them and tend them, making them bear fruit as he wished. This was the beginning of agriculture and a new type of people: the farmers.

(left) An example of making a pot by coiling clay, building up the sides and then smoothing the surface with a stone.

(right) Using a basket as a mould, the early pot makers pressed clay around the basket to get the shape of their pots.

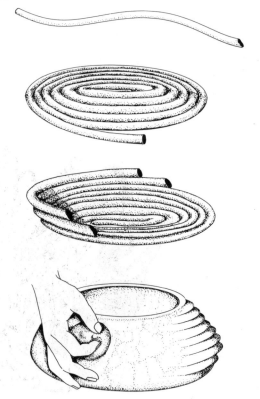

The farmers

Maize was so important to the Indians that many tribes had special gods for the crop. This is the Maize God of the Mayan Indians.

Pottery and farming usually came at the same time. Both required men to remain more or less in one place, for crops have to be tended and harvested, while clay deposits limit pot-making to one area. No longer would man simply follow the animals wherever they went—he would make them stay where he stayed. From these first basic steps of settlement all the world's great civilisations have sprung, for only when man settles down in a permanent home is there any chance of development.

We can say that farming began when man first tried to help nature do her work. In a period of dry weather, he may have carried water to a dying wild plant, or loosened the hard soil around its roots. Certainly he realised he could control growth when seeds fell from his basket. Often man left fruits on one wild bush so that it could drop seeds for the next season. All of these events led to regular farming. In about 3 000 BC American tribes in the highlands of Mexico were living on semi-wild plants such as peppers, beans, squash (pumpkin) and avocado pears.

The most important crop of the Americas was maize, or corn, which eventually became their staple diet. At first, maize was just a rough reed which grew in the Central American lands. After centuries of cultivation, man was able to improve the size of the cob and the fullness of the corn kernels. This crop was tended carefully, and the farmers produced a large number of varieties. These first American farmers spread the cultivation of corn to the north and south of Mexico. Maize brought great changes to the people of both continents and eventually tribes in most parts of the Americas had created ceremonies and even worshipped gods connected with the maize plant.

In Peru, the potato, which was first known as a wild, tuberous root, was developed by the people living in the fertile highlands of the Andes mountains. Over many years the potato was improved and became just as successful a crop as maize.

In the forests of the Amazon River Basin, in South America, the *manioc* or cassava was grown, and it became the most important crop for many tribal groups of South America, and later the Caribbean. It was found that crops could be cultivated not only as food, but as medicine and narcotics. One of these plants was tobacco.

As these crops developed, the farmers found new ways of making the earth produce more. If the soil was turned and watered, the crops would grow stronger. Weeds took energy away from the plants and special fields had to be cleared for planting. The farmers used fire to clear the land; today this method is known as 'slash and burn'. On steep hillsides, like those of the Andes farmers in Peru, there were problems in making fields on sloping land. When the rain fell the exposed soil was washed away and the crops were damaged. The people of Peru built stone terraces to keep the soil in place.

15

We have learned that farming brings settlement, and settlement means houses—homes for the farmers and their families, storage bins for crops, and huts for grinding corn. The first houses were nothing more than enlarged copies of the storage pits in the caves of the food-gatherers. In fact, many of the first houses were in the openings of caves, or against cliffs. Sometimes these people are called 'cliff dwellers'. These pit houses were round or square, several feet deep and lined with slabs of stone held up by posts. Roofs were made by means of slanting poles covered with bush and earth. American man was placing one stone on top of another when he built these houses. He was splitting and shaping stones to his own wishes. Stones make a wall,

(above) An Indian cliff dwelling in Arizona, North America.

(left) Fields and houses were tidily arranged by the early farmers of America, as can be seen in this painting of the Indian village of Secoton, Virginia.

(below) An Indian warrior from Florida.

walls make a house, houses make streets, and streets make cities. That is why it was such an important step when American man began to put stones together thousands of years ago.

Human beings are joined in families. The hunters and the food-gatherers roamed in families. The farmers clustered their houses together in families in the farming villages. The families were joined in kinship groups, the kinship groups in clans, the clans in tribes, and the tribes in nations. In all this we see a sense of order. There are important members of each family and clan. The other people listen to them and admire their wisdom and strength. These councils of respected members are accepted as leaders of the tribe. In this way we can see how the early settlements developed the first units of government in the Americas.

Warriors

It is natural that those people who settle in communities and obey laws, work hard and produce food will be more prosperous than others who lead a restless life, constantly on the move. While the first permanent communities were being established, the hunting and fishing tribes of the north and south still followed the game, and food-gatherers still moved with the seasons. But often there were times when opposing groups of hunters fought among themselves over hunting areas and clashed with wandering tribes who crossed their path. In many parts of the Americas tribal groups thrived by fighting and raiding other, more peaceful tribes, burning their settlements and plundering their stores of food and animals. Soon certain tribes got a reputation for their cruelty and ferocity in battle. They became regarded as warriors, men who simply lived for war.

The warriors of Mexico wore colourful battledress made up of bird feathers, carved wood and stone, and padded armour.

The Iroquois, Toltecs, Aztecs and Caribs are four warrior tribes from different parts of the continents. The Iroquois lived in the eastern forests of North America. Their families lived in permanent villages with houses built of wooden poles covered with bark. Iroquois warriors would go on the warpath after the council of the clan had decided to do so. Their method of battle was hand-to-hand fighting. To strike fear into their enemies, they would scalp some of their victims. They ate human flesh on ceremonial occasions, for it was believed that by eating the flesh of a brave warrior who had died under torture, one gained the dead warrior's courage.

These massive stone walls at the Ceremonial Baths at Tambo Machay in Peru were built by Incas and show their great skill in stone masonry.

The Toltecs and Aztecs were two of the warring tribes that roamed Central America. They were more advanced in their fighting methods and weaponry than many of the other people of the Americas. The Toltec warriors were armed with spear throwers, called *atlatls*, and darts and shields. They conquered people who were far more advanced in building and government than they were.

One of the last great warrior people of the Americas were the Aztecs. At first they were merely a primitive tribe that settled on small islands in Lake Texcoco, but within a hundred years they grew to dominate most of Mexico. We shall find out more about their kingdom in Chapter 3, but their rapid rise to power shows what skilful fighters they were and how important military organisation was to them. It is not surprising that military honours were given to those who showed prowess in war. The Aztecs believed that warriors were elevated to a special heaven after death.

The more advanced warrior kingdoms developed buildings to defend their towns and villages. The building materials depended upon the areas where these citadels were established. On the forested east coast of North America, warrior tribes made defences of stout tree trunks and heaped earth. In Mexico, the Aztecs defended their city by building it in the centre of Lake Texcoco. In the Andes mountains of Peru there were huge rocks in abundance. The Inca people skilfully cut the rocks so that they were able to fit firmly together, forming massive walls.

All over America developments were taking place. From the time the cliff-dwellers began to pile one stone upon the other thousands of years before, to the time in 1492 when Europeans first set foot on the Americas, some of the greatest buildings and early kingdoms of the world had developed on these two continents. As we find out more about the other civilisations we shall realise that each of the major races depended in some way on each other for their knowledge and new ideas in building, culture and government. But the outstanding thing about the continents of North and South America was that they developed independently. They were cut off for thousands of years from the influence of any other people. Asia, Europe, Africa knew nothing about these vast lands.

There is one more point to consider as we study the buildings, the fortresses, palaces, plazas and pyramids: the people of America knew nothing at all of the wheel, and almost nothing of beasts of burden. Horses, oxen, cows, goats and camels did not live on the continent. Only in the Andes were there llamas, which were tamed to carry loads. But, without the wheel, everything had to be dragged, hauled and hoisted. Even so, there arose among these hunters, fishermen, food-gatherers, farmers and warriors three great kingdoms of world history: the Maya, Aztec, and Inca kingdoms in America.

Aztecs

Maya

Incas

Pacifi

This map shows how the people of the Americas spread across the continents. The shaded areas show the three main empires of early America.

America

Atlantic Ocean

The Caribbean

America

Words to remember

The Americas	carcase	*atlatl*
Ice Age	archeologist	citadel
prehistoric	harpoon	canoe
Mongolian	yucca	farmer
glaciers	*manioc*	fisherman
bison	nomadic	warrior
tepee	tobacco	democratic

Things to do and discuss

1   Get a scrapbook for collecting extra information while you study this book.

2   Find pictures of icebergs, glaciers, snow and ice fields. Stick them in your scrapbook and make notes about them.

3   Have you ever been into a cave? If not, try to visit one and imagine how it would be to live in.

4   Draw a picture of a bison and find out if they still live in North America.

5   Make a blowpipe with a short length of bamboo. See how far you can blow a paper pellet out of it.

6   Write a short description of how to make a basket.

7   Why did the early Americans settle down in permanent dwellings?

8   Find out more about the Iroquois tribe of North America and write an essay about them.

2. The Maya

When man in the Americas turned to farming, a great change was made in his life-style. He developed a permanent home and formed a community of people who needed laws and systems of order. Agriculture in the Americas began in about 5 000 BC, somewhere in the highlands of Mexico. From this time the early American people began to develop social, religious and artistic life in their communities. Over hundreds of years these systems were improved to a very high level.

The first Americans to develop a very high level of culture were the Maya. Their civilisation was at its peak from about AD 350 to 800. This is known as the Classic Period. The Maya built over one hundred city states in the areas of Guatemala and Honduras, southern Mexico, and the peninsular of Yucatan. These towns were built in the midst of dense tropical jungle. Work was done with primitive tools and without the aid of beasts of burden or wheels. The Maya studied the stars and invented a calendar. They developed writing, sculpture and painting. There were priests and officials and a whole system of religion and government which ruled the people, who were scattered over this large area of Central America. Roads connected one town to another and Mayan canoes spread trade across the Caribbean sea.

Agriculture

Most of the Maya were farmers. Corn or maize was the main crop and was an important part of their religion, art and everyday life. It was such a sacred crop that prayers were offered to a young, beautiful corn god called Yum Kaax.

Mayan farmers did not own land separately, but worked their fields as one community. Each member of a tribe would be given a portion of cornland. The Mayan farmers cleared the forest trees by burning and cutting. The ground was broken with digging sticks and the grains of corn were planted. The whole family took part in weeding the fields and chasing away birds. When the corn was harvested the farmers had to give a portion to the priests and noblemen as a form of tax. The crop was stored in large underground storerooms or granaries called *chultunes*. The farmers' families lived in simple stone and thatch-roofed houses with one room and a doorway.

Beans, squash and pumpkins were grown in the cornfields, and chili peppers, sweet potatoes and sweet cassava were raised in separate

This map shows the Yucatan Peninsula, the Land of the Mayan civilisation.

20

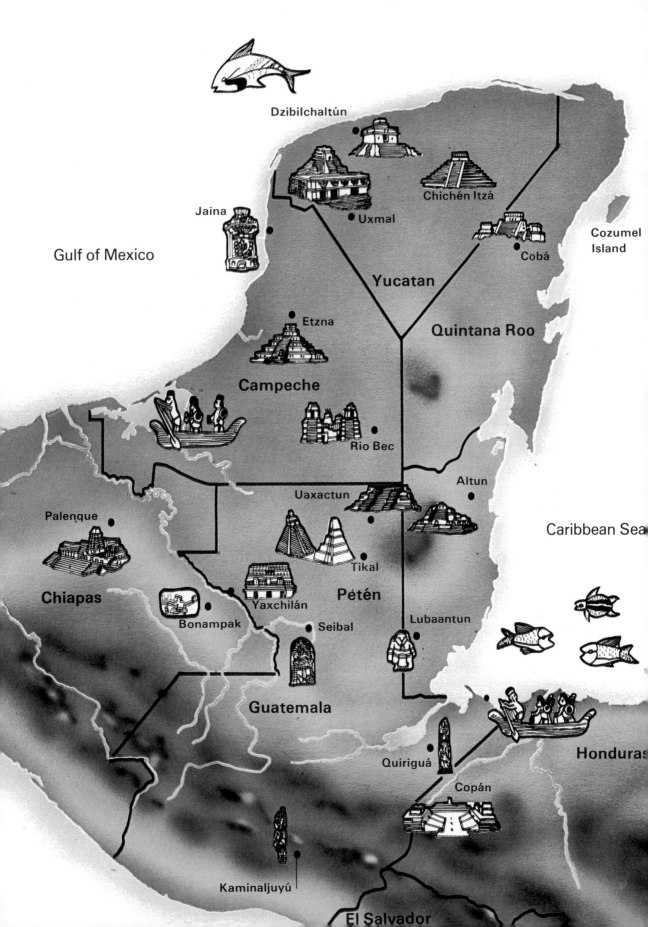

Dzibilchaltún

Chichén Itzá

Jaina

Gulf of Mexico

Uxmal

Yucatan

Cozumel
Island

Cobá

Etzna

Quintana Roo

Campeche

Rio Bec

Altun

Uaxactun

Palenque

Caribbean Sea

Chiapas

Tikal

Pétén

Yaxchilán

Bonampak

Seibal

Lubaantun

Guatemala

Quiriguá

Honduras

Copán

Kaminaljuyú

El Salvador

fields. Papayas, or pawpaws, and avocado pears were grown around their houses. Many other fruits grew wild and provided the Maya with bark, colouring, gum, wood and fruit for making many of the household things they needed. Cotton was grown in large quantities and was woven into fine material.

For all these crops to grow, the farmers required water. Huge reservoirs were built to hold water during the heavy rains. Wells, or *cenotes*, were dug, and from these water was carried to the fields. The Maya lived in fear of drought, and therefore they worshipped the rain god Chac, and they had great festivals to honour him.

Drawing water from a *cenote* and watering the fields.

Mayan society

The Mayan society and government were made up of many classes of persons. There was no single ruler over the whole mass of people who spoke the Mayan language. The land was divided into many city states ruled over by lords and noblemen. These men and their families dressed in expensive robes, covered with feathers and ornaments. Men and women wore cotton clothes dyed in many colours, and cloaks of feathers woven into cotton material. The chieftains wore huge headdresses of rare feathers, set with jade and other semi-precious stones. These important men were carried about on litters. Servants and slaves cooled them with fans and saw to all their needs.

The priests were also of the highest class. It was believed that they communicated between the men and the gods. The priests studied the stars and told farmers when to plant and when to reap. In turn the farmers had to supply the priests with everything they needed so as to keep favour with the gods. They gave the priests a share of their crops and the handcrafts which their families produced. Men had to help build the giant temples and carve huge stone blocks to decorate the walls. This was part of their duty to the gods.

Below the noblemen and priests there were many officers who organised the running of the city states. These men made sure everyone gave their portion of crops as taxes. They organised the division of land and work and kept records of the citizens of the land. Some were soldiers who trained villagers in the art of warfare. All these priests and officials were of the upper class and were not taxed.

The tax system of crops and labour supported the officials and priests. The people who provided the tax were the farmers and craftsmen who lived on the land around the main cities. At times of war they were expected to join the armies of their lord and defend their lands. Each man and woman was a member of one of the clans which made up the city states. The Mayan villagers were well dressed, although, of course, they did not have such fine decorations as the nobility. They tattooed their bodies and wore bone and semi-precious stone ornaments such as jade and topaz.

Most Maya flattened their foreheads, as a sign of beauty. This was done by the mothers when their babies were very young. Crossed eyes were also regarded as a sign of beauty and in order to develop this a ball was hung between the child's eyes.

At the top of the social pyramid was the leader of the state, who was both a high priest and a great lord. He was the *hulach uinic*, or 'true man'. He had full power over all the councils and officials of his city state. He inherited his position from his father. Below him were the chiefs of smaller towns within his state who carried out the *hulach uinic's* laws in their districts. These chiefs were called *batabobs*. Each *batabob* had a staff of officials to help him in his tasks.

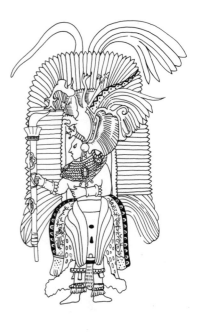

A Mayan ruling chief in his finery.

Mayan soldiers.

There was also a war chief or *nacom* who organised battles and raised armies. The men he led into battle were lightly armed. Their main weapons were spears and clubs, edged with obsidian stone. Slings were used with stones the size of eggs, and there were special spears (*atlatl*), as well as feathered shields.

After the maize had been harvested came the time for war. Women prepared food, such as corncakes and maize gruel, and porters followed the armies with food on their backs. Cities were often at war with one another, and enemy men were captured for use as slaves and often as sacrifices in the temples. Fighting was fierce and noisy. Drums, conch shells and whistles were beaten and blown to excite the soldiers. Houses were burnt and torn down, stones were thrown and groups of bowmen shot arrows into the enemy lines. Besides their shields, the only body protection used by the soldiers were tough, padded cotton jackets which covered the chest.

A Mayan woman weaver. One end of the loom is attached to the woman's waist, the other to a tree trunk.

Crafts

People skilled in many different crafts supplied the Mayan states with clothing, tools and household implements. Many were farmers as well as craftsmen, and in each city market place there was a lively trade and exchange in foodstuffs and cloth, bowls, axes, animals and other goods.

Cotton cloth was one of the important items of trade. Women sat at home weaving and dying the slender fibres on handlooms. Minerals and vegetable colours were used to make dyes. The cotton was picked from plants sown every year on the farms and from wild cotton trees which grew all over tropical America and the islands of the Caribbean.

The art of making beautiful feather costumes for the soldiers and nobility was highly developed by the Mayan women. The feather weavers made patterns with colourful plumes by twisting the feathers into the cotton threads as they worked on their looms. Feathers were brought from birds all over Yucatan. The most highly prized feathers were those of the sacred quetzal bird which lived high in the mountains. The quetzal had two bright green tail feathers which were of great value and were only worn by highest nobles in the land. The headdress of each soldier was carefully arranged on a helmet of wood or basketwork. Feathers were attached to weapons and shields. Bright feathered coats and costumes were worn by the priests. A ceremonial occasion in Mayan times must have looked like a carnival band in modern-day Trinidad!

Basketry and rope-making were also great arts. Rope was important in building, for men with rope wrapped around their shoulders pulled huge rock masses into position.

Pottery was well developed and was of many styles. By studying the pottery which remains in Mayan lands today, modern scientists can tell a great deal about the people who lived at the time. The shape and

An example of Mayan pottery: a dish with four legs.

decoration of the bowls and jars show how advanced the people were. All we see of the remains of Mayan pottery was done by women. It was the women who prepared the clay, shaped it and painted and fired the ornate containers of the Mayan civilisation. Besides containers, they also made charming model figures of people of all walks of life. By looking at this pottery we can see how the Maya dressed. The pictures painted on the pots also show us much of the Mayan myth and legend.

To decorate the pots, pounded stone and minerals were used. The main colours were brown, white, yellow, black and red. The pots held food and water. Sometimes the ashes of the dead were buried in jars. Incense was burnt in special clay containers.

The art of painting on clay also led to painting on the walls of special buildings. The Mayan artists painted large colourful frescoes on wet plaster. Although we cannot fully understand the symbols used by the Maya in recording their history, these pictures tell us many things about the Maya. Look at the wall painting of musicians on page 28.

A pyramid at Chichén Itzá.

Trade and the cities

With all of these goods being made and crops being grown, there was a brisk trade between the Mayan city states, and even further afield into lands which were not part of the Mayan empire. People came together to trade in large market places which were part of the city in their district. These cities were also the main religious centres of the area and here lived the lords and noblemen of the state. People came from all the surrounding farmlands to take part in religious festivals and official ceremonies, and to trade. The Maya built fine, straight roads to link the states and cities together. The photograph on page 25 shows us how marvellous these cities were!

There were many Mayan cities. The largest and most famous were Uxmal, Chichén Itzá, Tikal, Copán, Mayapán and Palenque. Even today, the buildings in these and other ruined cities amaze modern man. In Tikal, for instance, pyramids soar to 229 feet, towering above the jungle. These massive buildings were made of stone, cemented together with powdered limestone.

Thousands of people laboured to produce such buildings. They carried rubble and piled it high. Then stones were cut and dragged to the site. The blocks were hauled in place by simple muscle-power and then cemented together over the rubble. Such work took many years to complete. The pyramid of Kukulcán at Chichén Itzá, for instance, was built over a period of three hundred years.

The pyramids were really temples where the high priests went to worship and offer sacrifices to the sun and other gods which made up the religion of the Maya. Huge palaces were also built for the governors of the cities. Observatories were erected from which the priests and astrologers could study the stars. Arches were built over gateways, and everywhere stones were carved in the forms of gods, noblemen and symbols which told the history of the buildings and the city. Rulers were placed inside pyramids after death.

A temple at Tikal, one of the famous Mayan cities.

Huge ball courts were built, where the religious ball game, *pok-a-tok*, was played. This popular sport was rather like basketball. The ball was aimed at a stone ring set high in a wall. In some courts there was no ring, but players were padded and, being forbidden to use their hands, had to strike the ball with their hips to send it around the court.

Try to imagine one of these Mayan cities: there are lofty pyramids with shrines and temples at the top. Hundreds of steps lead upward to the sacred places where only priests can go. There are the great homes of the nobility and the market place is filled with people and goods from every part of the state. In the ball courts, priests are blessing players as they take part in the sacred game. Farmers and soldiers walk across the wide plazas, and noblemen are carried in curtained litters through the streets. Nearby, people are drawing water from the large *cenote*, and at the city gates officials are collecting taxes from each farmer as he enters with his goods.

A Mayan ball game in progress. Forbidden to use their hands, the players struck the ball with their hips, sending it around the court.

Religion and festivals

Religion was important in every part of Maya life, and festivals, games, music and dance were all part of religious ceremonies. The whole year on the Mayan calendar was divided into eighteen months, during each of which special festivals were celebrated.

Music was played in groups. The instruments were all percussion, as there were no stringed instruments in any of the early civilisations of America. The main rhythm came from a large wooden drum or *tunkul*. Tortoise shells and gourd rattles, conch shells, horns, wood and clay trumpets and pottery drums were some of the other instruments. Some dances included up to 800 performers who danced in formation with streamers and decorations.

The Maya worshipped gods of all kinds. They believed that some were in the underworld, some walked the earth, and others ruled the sky and the heavens. The beekeeper, the corn-grower, the fisherman, the warrior, the traveller, the merchant, even the comedian and the dancer, had their own gods. Statues were carved of all these gods and sacrifices of all sorts were placed at special temples and given to priests who guarded the shrines. All gods had to be treated with respect for they ruled all the forces and gifts of nature.

The priests knew when to observe special rituals and how these should be carried out. Sacrifices of crops, animals and humans were carefully regulated by the priests. The gods had to be nourished so that they could fight off the evils of drought, disease, or pests.

Blood was the most valuable sacrifice of all, and particularly an offering of a throbbing human heart. There were many forms of human sacrifice, but the tearing out of the heart was the most important. The victim was spread on his back across a sacred stone in the temple, the *nacom* priest slashed open the victim's chest, pulled out the heart and placed it in a special stone container before the image of the god they wished to satisfy. Blood was also drawn from various parts of the body and smeared over the idols. Often worshippers would draw blood from their own bodies. Another form of human sacrifice was made at water wells. The chosen victim was brought with great ceremony to the edge of the *cenote* and thrown in, after being weighted down with ornaments and stones. This occurred only during unusual times of drought, epidemic, or invasion.

Mayan musicians sing and beat time during a feast. This is a wall painting.

The calendar and writing

The order of time was a system which regulated the lives of all the Maya. There was a special time of year for everything. Dates had to be recorded to keep track of each event. To do this, the Maya developed a complex calendar of three circles, which kept track of days, months and years. The *haab* year was made up of eighteen months or periods. Each month was twenty days long. This added up to 360, so there were five additional days to each year, which were known as *vayeb*, or the unlucky days. This made up a year of 365 days. There was also a sacred calendar of 260 days. The third calendar recorded the number of days since the beginning of the Mayan era which was put at 3111 BC. No one knows why that date was important as a starting point in time for the Mayan people.

Mayans recorded their history by carving in stone. Here a Mayan man begs for mercy from a priest by passing a rope of thorns through his tongue.

With the calendar the priests could record the past eclipses of the moon and work out when it would happen again. They could note anniversaries and remember the dates of hurricanes, floods and other disasters. They believed that when certain dates came round again, the disasters would be repeated. Because the priests were among the few people who could explain the times of the calendar to the farmers, fishermen, hunters and builders, this added to their power and control over the people.

The Mayan high priest or *ahkin* taught the sons of noblemen how to write and reckon the months and the years. The Maya had a method of writing in symbols. Each symbol is called a 'glyph'. In every carving, wall painting and Mayan record, there are glyphs. But no one today can understand what they mean. Some people have been able to find the symbols for the days of the Mayan month, and the names of cities, but no one has yet been able to read a full sentence of Mayan glyph-writing. Besides carving the glyphs they also wrote on paper, but all except three pages of Mayan books have been destroyed. Therefore, much of their history remains a mystery.

One form of symbol which we can understand is Mayan numbers. It is quite a simple system. The bar (–) had a value of five and the dot (.) a value of one. These symbols were put together until number twenty was reached. Twenty was represented by a shell with a dot over it. The shell by itself represented zero. By using these symbols the Maya were able to count everything from years to cocoa beans and write down the amount to remember it. This may sound simple to us, but as a step in civilisation it is quite an achievement.

Although the Classic Mayan period ended at about AD 800, the Toltec Indians of Mexico took over most of the area and developed most of the Mayan way of life. This civilisation lasted up to 1194, when civil war broke out among the Mayan city states. Soon the forests had covered the beautiful cities; the temples, ball courts and palaces fell into ruin, and the whole system of trade and government collapsed. When the first visitors from Europe came to the Caribbean in 1492, the Mayan Empire was in its last stages of downfall.

The Mayan calendar.

(right) A stela, showing glyphs, almost twenty feet high, in Guatemala.

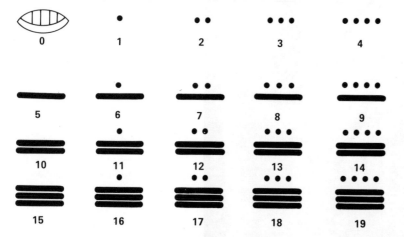

(left) Mayan numbers: the mollusc shell is the symbol for zero, the dot is one, and the bar is five.

30

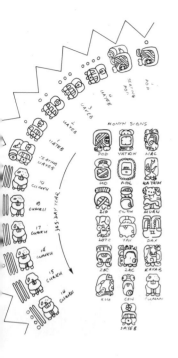

Words to remember

chultunes	reservoir	*tunkul*
glyph	granary	*nacom*
drought	jade	*cenote*
gruel	epidemic	topaz
Chac	incense	invasion
semi-precious	tattoo	*pok-a-tok*
vayeb	obsidian	*batabob*
sacrifice	*ahkin*	quetzal

Things to do and discuss

1 Do you think that the Mayan community system of work was a good thing?

2 Why was corn stored in *chultunes*?

3 What happens during a drought?

4 Collect pictures of pyramids in other parts of the world and paste them in your scrapbook. How do they differ from Mayan pyramids?

5 Imagine that you are a Mayan farmer taking pumpkins to sell in a city market. Write an essay describing what you do and see. Do not forget to pay your tax of two pumpkins to the tax collector!

6 Make a model of a Mayan pyramid and temple.

7 Explain why the priests were so powerful.

8 Find a picture of wall carvings of ancient Egypt. Compare these with Mayan glyphs.

3. The Aztecs

Towards the end of the thirteenth century, a brutal warrior tribe of Indians from the north of Mexico moved south and entered the beautiful Valley of Mexico. They were the Aztecs. Wherever these warriors tried to settle they were resisted by the already civilised American Indians who had established farms, villages and towns in the area. After years of war and struggle, the Aztecs made their capital on a small island in Lake Texcoco.

According to Aztec legend, the tribal elders had been guided to the place by their god, Huitzilopochtli. He had told them to look for an eagle perched on a cactus and eating a serpent. The eagle was the symbol of the sun and of the god. The tribal elders saw this sign on the island in Lake Texcoco, and they named their capital Tenochtitlán. That sign of the Aztec beginning remains the emblem of Mexico to this day.

One hundred years later, the Aztecs had conquered vast areas stretching from the coast of the Gulf of Mexico to the Pacific and as far south as Guatemala. The capital of Tenochtitlán was expanded by building out into the lake. Using strong reeds growing around the lake the Aztecs made rafts and filled them with earth. In these they grew their crops. These 'floating gardens', called *chinampas*, were anchored to the shallow lake bottom or towed to the islets on which the Aztecs lived. They added to Tenochtitlán in this way, filling in and extending the land, until the city took up a large section of the lake and housed about 200 000 persons. This became the centre of the Aztec empire. It was connected to the mainland by causeways which were well guarded

The sign given by the Aztec gods.

(below) An Aztec knife used for human sacrifice. Note the sharp stone blade. This stone, called obsidian, was used to make weapons and tools.

and easy to defend. It was a magnificent city of canals, plazas, markets, pyramids and temples, palaces, shops and fine homes.

Many civilised tribes had lived in Mexico before the Aztecs arrived. They too, had developed kingdoms and empires. Among them were the Olmecs, Maya, Miztecs, Huaxtecs, Totonacs, Toltecs and Tlaxcalans. Because the Aztecs were such powerful warriors, they were gradually able to defeat most of these other tribes and make their lands part of a greater Aztec empire. Another reason why the Aztecs rose to power in so short a period was because they adopted much of the culture and learning of the conquered tribes. The Aztecs added their own ideas and spread the culture throughout their empire. Soon the Aztecs were lords of the land. They were the leaders in government, religion and trade and controlled the lives of all the people living in the Valley of Mexico and beyond.

The ruler and his people

The supreme ruler of all the Aztec empire was a chief as well as a high priest. He was elected by a powerful council of chiefs and priests for his wisdom and record as a warrior and leader. He was the head of a loose federation of city states, all of which had to send tributes of food, merchandise and slaves to his palace at Tenochtitlán. The ruler of the Aztecs had as his title, 'the One Who Speaks', for on being elected the people believed that he became a priest-king who could understand and relate the signs of the gods.

(below right) Aztec priests perform a human sacrifice.

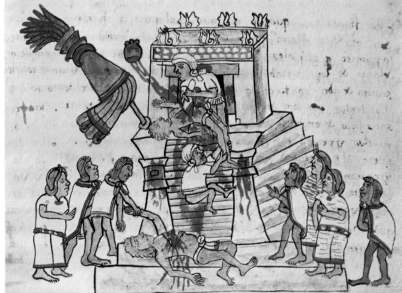

An Aztec floating garden, or *chinampas*.

Montezuma II, who was one of the last Aztec rulers. He reigned from 1466 to 1520, when he was defeated by the Spaniards at Tenochtitlán.

The ruler was surrounded by a court of noblemen and priests who lived in palaces, wore the best clothes and walked in sandals made of gold. The priests were most feared, for they were men of great knowledge who studied the stars, kept the temples and were in charge of the sacred human sacrifices. These were performed in much the same manner as the Maya, but the Aztec religion demanded human victims in far greater numbers. Every day human hearts and blood had to be offered before the images of the gods. To supply this need, men were captured and brought from all parts of Mexico. The priests matted their own hair with blood to satisfy the gods, and drew blood from themselves to smear over the statues.

Next in importance to the priests and nobles were the officials who administered the laws of the state, making sure tributes were paid, orders were carried out and seeing to all the general duties of government. Merchants were also in this rank. They travelled to all corners of the empire to do trade. Commerce was highly developed in the Aztec society. Merchants were also diplomats who did some government business as well as their own. They brought news from other cities and advised war captains about attacking new territories.

The craftsmen were next in rank. These artisans were sculptors of stone, jewellers who hammered precious metals and set gems, weavers of cotton, and masons who placed decorations and ornamental stone on temples and palaces.

These were followed by the commoners and peasants who tilled the land and reaped the crops. They lived in wood and thatch houses with mud floors and an open hearth fire for cooking. Their main food was corn, beans, peppers and fish. There was no grease for frying, so everything was either baked or boiled. The common man wore simpler clothes than the noblemen. Men had a simple loincloth and sometimes a cloak tied at one shoulder. The cloaks of the nobles were woven in bright colours and often covered in feathers. Women wore long skirts and simple blouses, or else ponchos.

The slaves made up the lowest rank. These were people captured in battle or people sold into bondage. They were treated as servants in the household of noblemen or laboured on building sites. But Aztec slaves were allowed to marry whom they pleased and their children were free citizens from birth.

The family and the community was given great respect in all ranks of Aztec society. All citizens were trained to honour their fathers and mothers, respect elders, live by good works and words and all sorts of other standards of good conduct. Although in war the Aztecs were far fiercer and more brutal than the Maya, we find that in their day-to-day habits they were much like the Maya and other developed tribes of early America.

Markets and cities

The city in each state was the centre of Aztec religion and trade. Farmers and craftsmen from surrounding areas came to sell their wares. A visitor to Tenochtitlán recalls that about 60 000 people would pass through the main market place each day. The articles for sale included gold, silver, jewels, feathers, mantles, chocolate, skins and leather, sandals and other hand-made products from roots and fibres.

The city of Tenochtitlán.

A visitor recalls that there were great numbers of male and female slaves, some of whom were fastened by the neck, in collars, to long poles. He continues:

'The meat market was stocked with fowls, game and dogs. Vegetable fruits, prepared food, bread, honey and sweet pastry were also sold here. Other places in the square were appointed to the sale of earthenware, wooden household furniture such as tables and benches, firewood, paper, copper, axes and working tools and wooden vessels highly painted. Numbers of women sold fish. The makers of stone blades were busy shaping them out of the rough material and merchants who dealt in gold had the metal in grains as it came from the mines. The entire square was enclosed in piazzas, under which great quantities of grain were stored, and where there were also shops for various kinds of goods.'

A gold ear plug, an example of Aztec gold work.

By looking at what was for sale in the markets we realise how much the Aztec people produced and how advanced they were in trade and in the development of their farms. As the Aztecs conquered more land they did not have to depend solely on the *chinampas* or 'floating gardens' for growing crops. Land was divided equally among the clans of the Aztec tribe. The *milpa*, or cornfields, were the most important farmlands. The gods of rain, and the goddesses of young corn and ripe corn, were worshipped as the corn grew. After harvesting, the corn was stored in large corn bins, and storerooms made of stone and baked clay. When needed, the grain was ground in stone mortars and used in cooking and making bread. In the same *milpa*, the Aztec farmer would also plant beans, squash, pumpkins and peppers. Sweet potato was grown in the warmer valleys. Cocoa was a highly prized drink and trade in cocoa beans was most valuable.

A nobleman being carried in a litter through the market place. In all the early American kingdoms noblemen were carried in this way.

The cities where these crops were sold were magnificent indeed. Many of the buildings and pyramids remain today. The Temple of the Sun at Teotihuacan was the largest pyramid in Mexico. It was 216 feet high and covered ten acres of land. There were many others like it, but not as tall. Steps rose steeply to platforms at the top where temples stood. Many of them were built even before the Aztecs arrived in Mexico.

The palaces of the lords were spacious. Wood carvings and fresh flowers adorned the stone walls. Mats were spread out for sitting on and aqueducts of carved stone and clay carried water into the buildings from outside the cities. The causeways which connected Tenochtitlán to the banks of Lake Texcoco were broad and straight. To send messages from one city to another the Aztecs had a system of runners who ran in relays and in this way covered long distances. The nobles were carried about on litters and because there were no beasts of burden, porters transported all the goods on their backs across the rugged land.

The sunstone or Aztec calendar.

(left) Montezuma's headdress, an example of Aztec featherwork.

Religion, war and festivals

Religion and war were closely linked in the Aztec empire. Blood was needed for the gods, and victims were needed to provide the blood. Therefore, Aztec warriors did not only conquer tribes to increase the empire, but to take prisoners. The god who demanded human sacrifice most was Huitzilopochtli, or 'Lord Smoking Mirror', the Hummingbird Wizard and God of the Sun. The Aztecs believed that if he did not receive nourishment he would be unable to rise at dawn and the Aztec nation would be destroyed.

But the Aztecs also worshipped another god, Quetzalcoatl, 'the Feathered Serpent'. He was the god of learning and taught men agriculture, arts, and industry. These two important gods were for ever locked in battle for power. Once, Quetzalcoatl was beaten and driven away. He went east across the sea, vowing that one day he would return to take revenge. As we learn more about the history of Mexico, we shall find out that this legend helped to cause the destruction of the Aztec empire.

There were many lesser gods. Plants and people had gods and each function, be it grinding corn or walking, had its god or goddess. The gods of evil fought the gods of goodness and the priests studied all their signs. These priests directed the whole complicated religious system and told the people how to order their lives to suit the various spirits. This made the priests most powerful.

Every able-bodied Aztec was a warrior. He fought as well as farmed. Women tended the crops while the men were at battle. Aztec armies were, like the Mayan, very colourful. Costumes and headgear of animal skins and plumes were supposed to frighten the enemy. They painted their faces. Shields of wood and feathers bore the crest of their clan. The most feared weapon was the *maquahuitl*, a sword

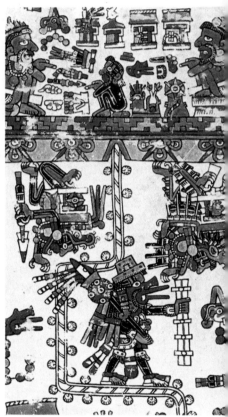

The God Quetzalcoatl from the Codex Zouche. At the top, Quetzalcoatl sits among the temples. In the lower part of the picture he is seen descending to earth by means of a rope ladder. He wears a high-crowned hat.

37

with several blades of sharp stone. There was also a sort of tomahawk. Bows and arrows, javelins and spears were also used. Like the Maya, the Aztec soldiers were experts at slinging stones.

Warlords led the mass of warriors into battle. If they were victorious they burned the temple of their enemy as a sign of victory. The conquered people could keep their own dress, manners and chieftains, but every six months they had to give tributes of food and craftswork to the Aztecs.

Festivals were also part of religion. There were many gods to worship and celebrate, each with their special days of festival. Musicians and performers came out to play, sing and dance. One amazing ceremony was the dance of the flyers. Men dressed as birds climbed to the top of a tall pole to imitate birds. A drummer provided music while everyone watched. Jugglers also performed on feastdays and jesters entertained the nobles. Musical instruments were wooden trumpets, drums, gourd rattles and conch horns. Like the Maya, the Aztecs had elaborate ball courts. Chiefs and priests sat in special areas to watch strong players hitting the ball into a stone ring.

Writing and the calendar

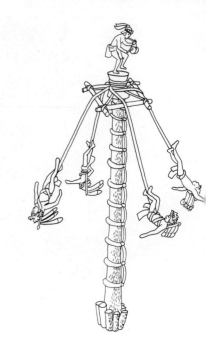

The dance of the fliers.

All advanced people have some form of paper, some form of writing, and some form of literature. The Aztecs had all of these. Paper was made from the bark of the wild *Ficus* tree. The bark was cut in large strips and beaten into rolls of paper and then folded to make books. Most of the high cultures of Central America made paper.

Writing was in the form of glyphs, or symbols, and most of the Aztec books were written to keep information. There were records of dates, of families, trials and tributes. All of this was carefully set down by the priests and writing artists. Whole libraries of these books existed in Aztec Mexico, but soon after the Spanish conquerors arrived in 1519, these were destroyed. Christian priests did not understand the writing, and thought the books were evil. They burned hundreds of Aztec books and only about fourteen remain today.

Aztec warriors with their weapons, headgear and shields.

The Aztec calendar was very much the same as that of the Maya. Huge circular stones, marked with all the signs for the days, months and years were carved. These were set into the walls of palaces and temples and from them priests judged the special days both past, present and future. Time and dates were of great concern to the Aztecs. All their work, lives, hopes and fears were based on the will of the gods and the special dates set down in their stone calendars.

What an outstanding people the Aztecs were! They had risen from being wandering warriors to powerful and learned city folk within four hundred years. But their fall was even more sudden than their rise to power. In 1519, at the peak of their civilisation, Mexico was visited by conquerors from across the seas. These people were far more powerful than the Aztecs. By 1525 the empire of Mexico was in ruins.

Words to remember

chinampas	relay	porters
canal	Quetzalcoatl	shield
plaza	*maquahuitl*	juggler
pyramid	commerce	tribute
Tenochtitlán	cocoa	gourd
milpa	litters	ball court

Things to do and discuss

1 How did the Aztecs gain power in Mexico?

2 Why do you think the Aztec craftsmen were respected?

3 Why did the Aztec warriors not fight all the year round?

4 The Aztecs carved many fine statues. Look for examples of their work in other books.

5 Describe how you would build a *chinampas*.

6 How did the temple priests get a regular supply of human victims for their sacrifices?

7 If you had lived in Tenochtitlán, which class of person would you like to have been and why?

8 Draw an Aztec soldier in your scrapbook.

4. The Incas

Far to the south of Mexico, almost in the centre of the Andes mountain range, there was another early American empire: the Inca. The Incas, like the Aztecs, were latecomers. When they began spreading across the land they met civilisations which had been there for hundreds of years before them. But by the strength of their armies, the Incas overcame these earlier people and developed an empire which stretched for more than 2 500 miles along the west coast of South America. This land was made up of cold mountains, tropical jungles, hot deserts and steep gorges and canyons. But even on this rough terrain the Incas found towns and fields peopled by many different tribes. They had lived in the area for over a thousand years before the Incas arrived. Among them were the Chavin, Mochica, Paracas and Chimu.

For years these tribes had built houses and developed systems of government for themselves. By carving channels in the hillsides and setting down narrow canals of stone, they brought water from rivers into dry wasteland. Where the land was too steep they made terraces to hold the soil. On these terraces they planted fields of potato and maize. Where farming was impossible these tribes put llamas to graze. Roads were built among the mountains. Buildings were made of sturdy blocks of stone set firmly together.

Llamas. These were the only beasts of burden known to the people of ancient America. The llama is a distant relative of the camel and was used for carrying loads and for eating.

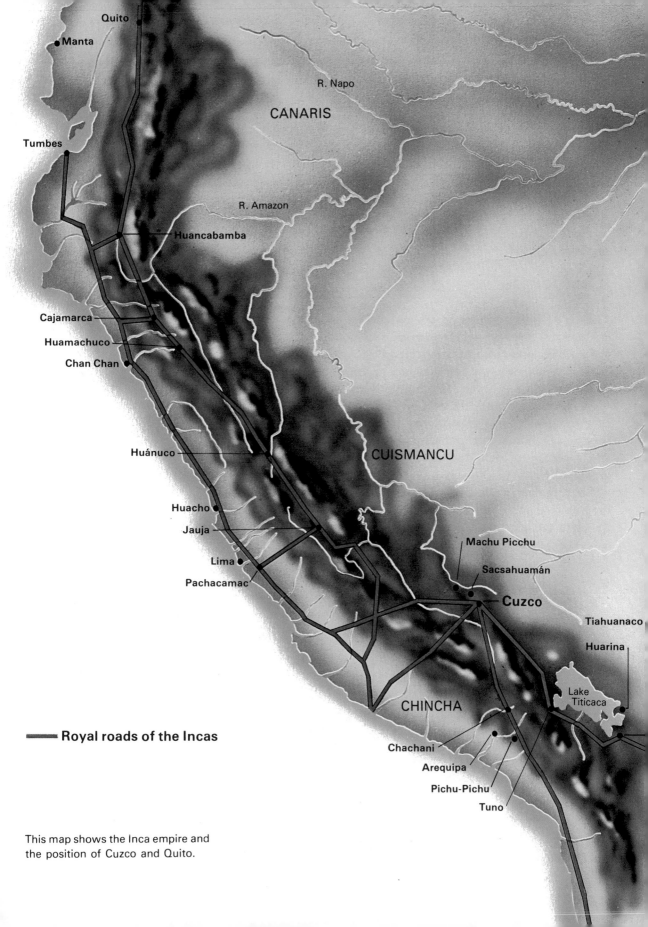

Quito
Manta
R. Napo
CANARIS
Tumbes
R. Amazon
Huancabamba
Cajamarca
Huamachuco
Chan Chan
Huánuco
CUISMANCU
Huacho
Jauja
Machu Picchu
Lima
Sacsahuamán
Pachacamac
Cuzco
Tiahuanaco
Huarina
Lake
Titicaca
CHINCHA
Chachani
Arequipa
Pichu-Pichu
Tuno

Royal roads of the Incas

This map shows the Inca empire and
the position of Cuzco and Quito.

At first the Incas were probably potato farmers and llama herders living in the highlands. As they searched for more fertile land they defeated other tribes. Their first ruler, Manco Capac, founded the capital city, Cuzco.

The valley of Cuzco was very fertile and it had been farmed for two thousand years before the Incas arrived. From Cuzco, the Incas developed their empire to the north and south. Gradually they became the most powerful tribe in that part of South America. The Incas believed that the first Inca, Manco Capac, had been created by the Sun God. Each ruler was called Inca, and from him the people received their name. The rulers were believed to be direct descendants of the Sun God.

The people

The Incas lived together in communities which shared the land, animals and crops among themselves. Each community was a clan or *ayllu* which was ruled by an elected leader, *mallen*, directed by a council of old men who gave advice to the clan. Men and women worked together in teams, farming potatoes and corn.

All over the empire there were officials who made sure that everything was being done correctly. There were, for instance, inspectors of roads, keepers of records, officers for the upkeep of bridges, and governors of each district. The life of the Incas was very well organised.

The Supreme Inca was both a king and a god. Being a descendant of the Sun God and Creator, everything belonged to him. The land and the earth was his. The gold, called 'the tears of the sun', and silver 'the tears of the moon', also belonged to him. Around him were nobles and

Manco Capac, the first Inca ruler, as pictured by a European artist. Manco Capac is said to have led the Inca people to the Valley of Cuzco where he founded the Inca empire around the year 1200.

Inca officials: **a** a provincial governor, **b** an administrator, **c** a *quipucamayac*.

officials who did his will. The whole state was supported by taxes taken from each *ayllu*. Everyone benefited from these taxes, for they were used to build roads, bridges, canals, towns and terraces for growing crops. Corn, potatoes and dried llama meat were set aside in storehouses in case of emergency.

Weapons for the army were also provided by the state. They were kept in armouries so that when it was decided there would be war, the men of the district would be called together and weapons were distributed among them. There were clubs, spears and shields. The soldiers wore helmets of wood and straw. The most popular weapon was the sling.

The buildings and cities

The Incas were great builders. The whole Inca system of government made sure that people were working all the time, trading goods, farming, making handicrafts and buildings roads, bridges and houses.

Huge boulders were carefully cut into shape so as to fit firmly together. These were drawn from stone quarries and pulled into place by men working wooden levers and rollers to shift them. No one can explain how the stonemasons were able to chip each mass of rock so neatly that each would fit into the other like bits of a jig-saw puzzle.

By setting these stones firmly together the Incas could build on the steep hillsides just as well as on the flat plains. Like the tribes before them, the Incas made terraces to prevent the soil being washed away by rain. On the earth between each terrace crops were grown. Houses were also built on terraces of this kind. Some towns, such as Machu Picchu, were built entirely on mountainsides, complete with streets, plazas, water canals and temples.

Worshipping the Sun at the Sun Temple, Cuzco.

This picture of Inca farmers at work in their terraced fields shows how the fields were irrigated by canals.

43

The ruins at Macchu Pichu, Peru.

An Inca bridge across a gorge.

To connect these towns there was a vast network of roads reaching to all parts of the empire. These were also built of stone and cut into cliff-sides. Steps were built along mountain roads and bridges made it easier to cross deep gorges. These bridges are one of the most remarkable achievements of the Incas. Stone pillars were erected high up on each side of the gorges. Ropes were strung across from each group of pillars to create a 'swing bridge'. By tying lengths of ropes in the form of railings and placing firm wooden planks along this ropeway, travellers could cross the dizzy heights to the other side. It must have been rather frightening, but it was much easier than winding one's way down to the very bottom of the gorge and up the other side. Only very heavy loads were not taken across such bridges. To ensure that the rope bridges were always safe, there were special inspectors of bridges who were responsible for getting the bridges repaired. There were two other types of bridge. Reed boats were tied together across wide rivers to form pontoon bridges and stone slabs were placed together over smaller streams.

44

To travel over large areas of water the Incas used reed boats made of lengths of swamp reeds tied firmly together. Boats like these are still used by descendants of the Incas on Lake Titicaca between Peru and Bolivia. The ancient Incas also used large rafts made of logs of balsa wood. These rafts had sails, and a rough deckhouse of palm leaves.

The Incas had a system of sending messages that was faster than any other such system in America. Runners were stationed at points along each road. They ran in relays and passed on messages for hundreds of miles. The couriers or runners were called *chasqui*. They ran with a club and slingshot to protect themselves, and carried information or light parcels from one running post to the next.

We can see that the Incas developed many fine things, but it is strange that, unlike the Maya and Aztecs, they had no form of writing. There was, however, a very clever method of recording figures and amounts. All the Inca records were kept on bits of knotted string. Each knot meant something and represented a certain amount. These string records were called *quipi*. Amounts of property, foodstores, gold,

This photograph shows present-day reed boats on Lake Titicaca. These boats are like those used by the Incas on this lake.

45

silver, soldiers and people were all recorded in this way. Other strings were tied to the main string and each string had a different meaning. Naturally there were only special people who could work out what the *quipi* recorded. If we saw one of these information sheets of the Incas we would think it was simply a mass of knotted string. Modern computer machines relay information on strips of paper pierced with holes. Each group of holes in the paper means something special, and so it was with the knots on the Inca *quipi*.

The Inca empire had no connection with the other early American empires in Mexico and Yucatan. Their knowledge of the world did not go that far. But on their own the Incas built up all the systems and ways of living within the empire. The supreme god was the Sun God, but there were many lesser gods who were worshipped by different groups of Incas. The religion and government kept peace and order across the empire. Because of the runners and district officials, a check could be kept on all parts of the land. If there was trouble in any of the districts an army would quickly be sent to the area. The tax system ensured that every Inca got his or her share of food and clothing, and in this way order was kept for many years.

The *quipi*, the method by which the Incas recorded figures on knotted strings. Each knot and the space between them represents varying amounts and distances.

Inca rulers handed their position from father to son. To make sure the sacred position of Supreme Inca remained within the family, the Inca rulers often married their sisters.

Once, in 1527, a civil war broke out between two sons of the Supreme Inca over which of them should control the empire. This seriously divided the Inca people. The two princes, Atahualpa and Huascar, fought with each other's armies until Huascar was finally defeated. But at this same time European explorers and conquerors were moving south from Mexico. The divided empire was weak and, when the two forces met in battle, the Incas with their slings and clubs were no match for the Europeans' guns and horses. As all the organised Inca systems collapsed the great South American empire came to an end.

Atahualpa, the last Supreme Inca.

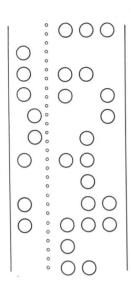

A modern strip of computer paper. Each group of perforations represents numbers and letters which are decoded by being passed through a computer.

Words to remember

terrace	inspector	raft
herder	elected	*chasqui*
Cuzco	helmet	balsa
ayllu	gorge	*quipi*
mallen	pontoon	civil war

Things to do and discuss

1   Why is irrigation important for growing crops?

2   Why did the Incas make terraces on the hillsides? Do you know of any places in your country where there are stone or grass terraces on the hillsides?

3   How did the Inca officials help to maintain law and order in the empire?

4   Why was road-building so difficult in Peru?

5   Draw a picture in your scrapbook of a pontoon bridge.

6   Do you run relay races at school? Get together with other pupils in your class to relay a verbal message around the playing field as fast as you can. Compete with other teams. Make sure each team member passes on the original message without getting it mixed up!

7   If you had to choose between the Maya, Aztecs and Incas, which of these three civilisations would you have preferred to live under? Give reasons for your choice.

5. The Islands

I f we look at a map of the Caribbean region we can imagine the Caribbean Sea to be a very large lake. About three-quarters of this lake is bordered by the mainland of America, curling from Guyana and Venezuela, through Panama, Honduras, Belize, Mexico and North America to the tip of Florida. The other side of this imagined lake is bordered by islands. These islands curve from Trinidad to Cuba and on towards the Bahamas in a gentle arc. Each island is like the link in a chain, or the beads of a necklace. These are the Antilles or Caribbean islands. The largest are in the north of the chain, and the smallest make a line to the east. Therefore we can easily divide the chain of the Caribbean islands into two—the Greater Antilles (including Cuba, Hispaniola, Jamaica, and Puerto Rico), and the Lesser Antilles (from the Virgin Islands to Grenada).

The people who wandered southwards down the American continent ventured along the Andes and eastwards into the tropical jungle region of the large southern continent. After thousands of years some of these tribes came to Trinidad and the first islands of the Lesser Antilles. They saw that beyond them lay other islands, and gradually these tribes of Amerindians moved up the chain and settled in these new lands.

But not all of the islands were the same. Some had tall, steep, forested mountains and swiftly flowing streams; others were flat and

(right) The Pitons of St Lucia in th
Windward Islands are the peaks o
extinct volcanoes.

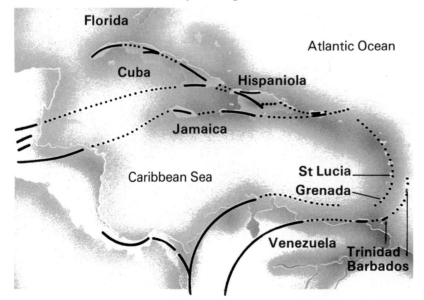

The mountain ranges of the Caribbean. Note how the island mountains follow in lines from the mountain ranges on the mainland continent.

dry. Some had black sand beaches, and some were ringed with golden coral sand. However, each island was very beautiful. How did these natural features come about? How were these islands made? To find out we have to go back millions of years.

The formation of the islands

One hundred million years ago we would not have recognised the Caribbean region as it is today. The land mass of South America stretched much further north, reaching almost as far as Grenada. Deep down on the sea bed the first mountains were being formed by pressures in the earth's crust.

The earth folded and cracked, pushing some sections upwards, while others plunged deeper. In this way the mountains which lie in a chain from Mexico to Puerto Rico and from Central America through Jamaica to Hispaniola, were thrust upwards. Meanwhile, the rivers of South America were bringing down masses of mud and silt which spread over the sea floor of the Caribbean. All of this action took place between 50 and 70 million years ago.

Another great period of disturbance occurred 26 million years ago, when the folding of the land created the mountains of the Greater Antilles. Slowly the islands rose out of the ocean depths, covered in the rich deposits from the South American rivers. This was the basis of the soil on our islands today. By this time the islands of the Greater Antilles were well established, but in the Lesser Antilles, violent volcanoes were still creating new islands.

Volcanoes   Most of the islands of the Eastern Caribbean were built up by volcanic action. A volcano is a mountain formed by materials from beneath the earth's crust. The earth's crust is made up of rock thirty miles thick and beneath this there is a molten material called *magma*. When magma forces its way to the surface it is called *lava*.

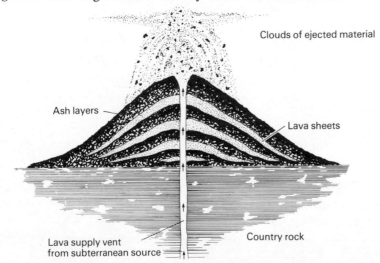

Clouds of ejected material

A volcano erupting.

Ash layers

Lava sheets

Lava supply vent from subterranean source

Country rock

Lava pouring from the *vent* of a volcano builds up a cone-shaped mountain. Ash is also blown from the vent, and when it falls it forms layers on top of the lava and helps to build the volcano higher.

This is what happened in the Eastern Caribbean in the islands from Saba to Grenada. Volcano erupted upon volcano and slowly the mountains rose through the ocean depths. The islands formed in this way are called 'oceanic islands' because they come from the ocean floor. This line of Caribbean islands is known as the Volcanic Caribees, or the 'first-cycle islands'. The group between Guadeloupe and St Vincent is known to be of recent origin because there are still semi-active volcanoes, peaceful craters and *fumeroles*, or hot springs.

Limestone islands   There are other islands, such as Barbados, the Bahamas and some of the Leeward islands, which are different from the volcanic islands in the inner arc of the Caribees. These islands are lower and have much less rugged surfaces. They are made of limestone rocks. There are many different types of limestone rock, but coral limestone is made up of the remains of coral reefs. Reefs are made of the remains of tiny sea creatures called 'polyps'. These are surrounded by shells which remain piled up when the coral polyps die. After the Antilles rose above the surface of the ocean, the islands were eroded by wind, rain and the sea. This broke down the tops of the steep rock formations, creating valleys, ravines, gulleys and caves. The volcanic material formed black sand beaches, while in the limestone islands, golden sand beaches made of powdered coral ringed the shores.

Barbados is made of coral limestone and is, therefore, very flat. Sometimes limestone is exposed on old sea cliffs like this one, which was formed when the island rose out of the ocean millions of years ago.

51

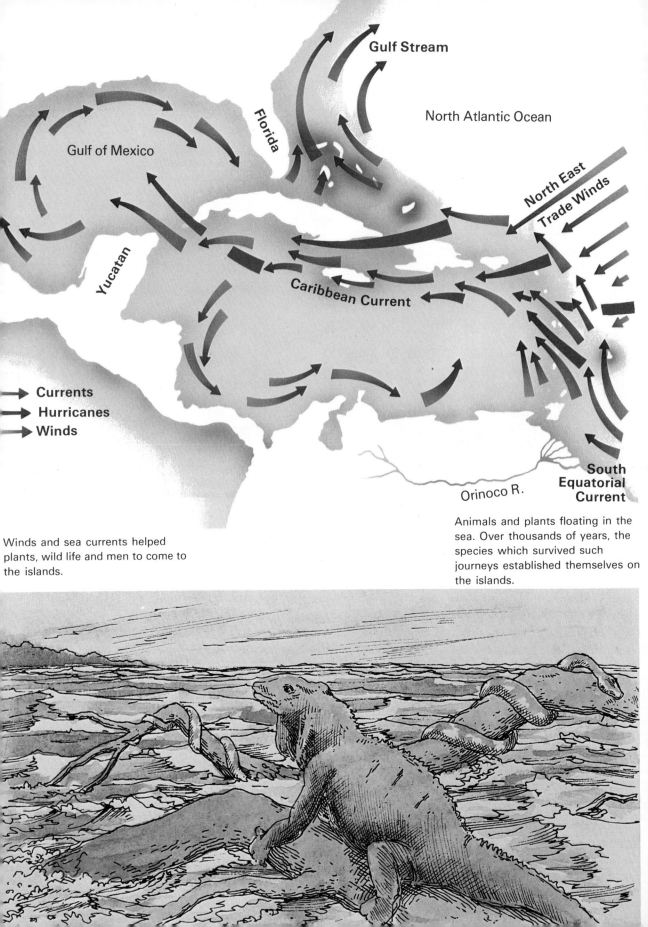

Gulf Stream

North Atlantic Ocean

Florida

Gulf of Mexico

North East

Trade Winds

Yucatan

Caribbean Current

South
Equatorial
Current

Orinoco R.

→ Currents
→ Hurricanes
→ Winds

Winds and sea currents helped
plants, wild life and men to come to
the islands.

Animals and plants floating in the
sea. Over thousands of years, the
species which survived such
journeys established themselves on
the islands.

Life

Even before all this violent activity was over, plants were taking root in the rough soil. How could the plants have reached these islands? The ocean currents played a part in transporting them. The Antilles lie in the path of the South Equatorial Current. This flows from West Africa to South America, where a branch of it mingles with the Orinoco River and then flows into Caribbean waters.

Fruits and seeds can remain fertile in spite of long ocean journeys, for around most seeds there is a dry husk which enables them to stay afloat for long periods. The South Equatorial Current carried plants and even small animals from the Guianas in South America to the shores of the Antilles. Even after many months in the sea, seeds were able to germinate when washed up on fertile ground. And once a plant has taken root on the seashore the seeds it produces are easily dispersed inland.

The next time you go near the sea, walk along the shore and count how many types of seed you find washed up on the beach.

An iguana.

Birds also carried seeds to the islands. Many varieties of bird migrated north and south along the Caribbean chain from the mainland continents.

One reason why the Caribbean islands have so few animals, apart from birds, is because of the ocean currents. No large mammal or reptile can survive for long in the sea, and therefore the only wildlife able to make the journey to the islands were insects and small reptiles. Large logs and tangled branches floated in the currents and on them often clung lizards, snakes, land crabs and other life.

The largest reptiles to arrive on the islands were snakes and iguanas. Snakes vary from island to island. Some are small and harmless, others are poisonous. There are also large boa-constrictors. The largest mammals include the agouti, manicou and coney. Although these mammals originally came from the mainland of South America, it is believed that they were brought to the islands by man.

And man himself was helped by the natural forces of the winds and currents. The Amerindians who came to the islands in their canoes were assisted on their way by the South Equatorial Current. The

Europeans who came much later were helped by the winds which blew towards the Eastern Caribbean from across the Atlantic. As the Europeans developed trading routes between the Caribbean and Europe, they found these winds so helpful that they called them the Trade Winds.

Hurricanes can be very destructive. Winds of up to 200 miles an hour sweep off the Atlantic Ocean towards the Caribbean area.

But the Caribbean also lies in the path of destructive hurricanes which sweep across the islands, wrecking everything in their path. Once a hurricane begins to form, wind speeds soon reach 75 miles an hour and occasional gusts near the centre may reach 200 miles an hour. The centre itself is calm. No one can predict accurately what course a hurricane will take, though most develop over the Atlantic Ocean, travelling in a westerly direction into the Caribbean and then curve northwards. The destruction caused by hurricanes has been recorded from the earliest days of Caribbean history.

Four thousand years ago no human being had yet set foot on these islands. Forests had grown unhindered down to the water's edge. The streams abounded in fish and eels, and across the silent valleys flew birds of many kinds. The coral reefs fringing the islands teemed with schools of bright fish. After millions of years of formation, the Caribbean was at peace; yet its recorded history had not begun. From the coast of South America that had brought the islands their wildlife and vegetation, there was to come a new creature: Man, the first West Indians.

Words to remember

arc   *vent*   current

Lesser Antilles   oceanic islands   agouti

Greater Antilles   *fumerole*   manicou

volcano   coral   Trade Winds

magma   polyps   hurricane

Things to do and discuss

1 In which part of the Caribbean do you live? Is it a volcanic or limestone area, and what proof can you find to show how it was formed?

2 Write an essay on some of the volcanic eruptions which have occurred in the Caribbean.

3 Find pictures of a coral sand beach and a volcanic sand beach for your scrapbook.

4 Name five birds which live in your country.

5 Collect five types of seed from along the seashore or river bank.

6 Draw a snake in your scrapbook. Are there any snakes where you live?

7 Describe what your home town or village may have been like before man ever came to your country.

6. The Arawaks

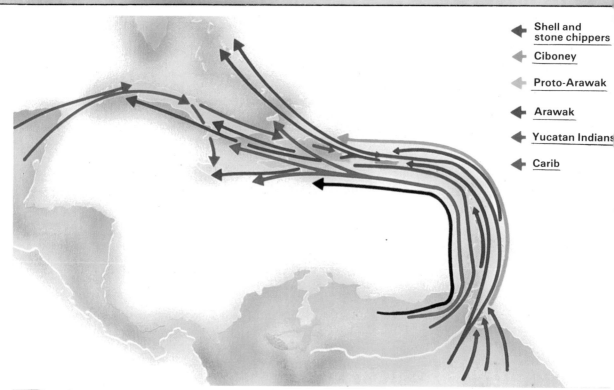

Shell and
stone chippers

Ciboney

Proto-Arawak

Arawak

Yucatan Indians

Carib

How man came to the islands.
Waves of Indian tribes travelled over
the sea from the north and south at
different times during a period of five
thousand years.

P eople had been living on the islands of the Caribbean for
hundreds of years before Columbus arrived there in 1492. We
know that when he arrived there were two groups of
Amerindians on the islands, the Arawaks and the Caribs.

To find out about the other people who had lived in the Caribbean
before that time is more difficult. All that is left is the pottery, carved
stones and shellwork which they left behind in their settlements. Over
the years these were covered by earth, and today archaeologists dig
through the layers of soil to study the pieces which remain. Often it
takes several years of study, but, very gradually, by piecing all of their
information together, the archaeologists can tell us about the first
Caribbean people.

From these studies we now know that six cultural groups of people
came from the mainland of South and Central America to settle in the
islands. All of them were Amerindians.

Archaeologists have found out that the first group of Amerindians
came to the islands from the mainland where Belize and Yucatan

(right) Some stone tools used by the
early settlers of the Caribbean.

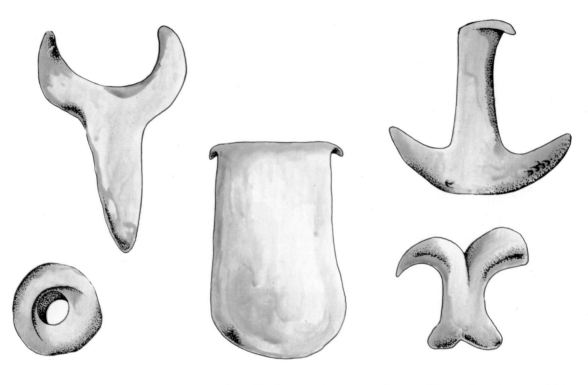

are today. Look at your map and you will see that they would have first arrived on the islands of Jamaica and the Greater Antilles. These people knew nothing about the art of making pottery, which is called ceramics. We therefore call them pre-ceramic people. They did, however, make gouges from shells, and broke stones into shapes which were used as tools.

Then from Venezuela there came another pre-ceramic people, called the Ciboneys. They first arrived at the islands of Trinidad and Grenada and moved northwards from island to island in their wooden canoes. They made long, narrow, stone axes and, like the first group, they were food-gatherers who lived on wild fruit, fishing and hunting. They lived in caves.

The third group of Amerindians to come to the islands were also from Venezuela. But these made pottery and practised agriculture. They were more culturally advanced than the Ciboneys.

These people were followed by the fourth group—the Arawaks. The Arawaks came from the northern banks of the Orinoco River and moved up the islands of the Lesser Antilles in their canoes. Eventually, they reached as far north as Cuba and the Bahama islands. The Arawaks were skilful at working pottery, and also grew and wove cotton.

Then came the Caribs, a tribe of warriors who moved up the Lesser Antilles, raiding the peaceful Arawaks and taking over their settlements.

Last of all there came people from Yucatan who settled in the large islands of the Great Antilles. They introduced ball courts rather like those used by the Maya Indians. But of all these six groups, the Arawaks and the Caribs are the most important. Between them they dominated the islands of the Caribbean for two thousand years, from about 500 BC to AD 1 500.

We also know the most about these Indians because of the accounts of their houses, canoes and way of life. Columbus and other Spanish explorers could write and were able to leave these descriptions. Spanish and French missionaries also took great interest in the lives and language of the Indians and left records of their culture. Let us now first look at how the Arawaks lived on the islands.

Farmers and fishermen

About 1 000 BC, there lived on the lower banks of the Orinoco River in South America a brown-skinned, peaceful and easy-going people. They were the Arawaks. They hunted small animals, fished and cultivated *manioc*, or cassava. The Arawaks made canoes from the trunks of trees. These held as many as fifty people, sometimes more.

Around 500 BC, the Arawaks set out in their canoes from the mouth of the Orinoco and moved towards the islands. Before them lay Trinidad and Grenada. The movement of the Arawaks occurred northwards and was developed in stages. Because of the means of their navigation, they had to land on each island as they travelled, and they often settled for a number of years before moving on.

Aboard the canoes were men, women and children. They carried with them supplies of food, animals and pottery. Fruit like the guava was brought in this way to the Antilles. Supplies of *manioc*, sweet potatoes (called *batata*), yams, corn and cotton were wrapped in packages of leaves and tied with cord from the bark of trees. Animals were also taken. The agouti, a large rodent, and the *manicou*, or opposum, were most probably carried to the islands by the Arawaks in their canoes.

For a thousand years, waves of these people ventured up the Antilles. On they moved, along the small islands of the Windwards and Leewards, past the Virgin Islands, and into the Greater Antilles, Puerto Rico, Hispaniola, Cuba, Jamaica and the Bahamas. After a time there were thousands of Arawak villages throughout the length of the Caribbean chain.

A cassava plant and its starchy tu
which was so important to the
Arawaks and Caribs.

The Arawaks introduced agriculture, permanent villages, the idea of chiefs and noblemen, and ceremonies which involved sacred images. The Arawak villages were scattered along the coasts and near the rivers. The houses or huts, made of wooden frameworks of firmly tied posts and built to withstand fierce hurricanes, were grouped roughly together around an open square. The roofs sloped sharply to let the rain run off quickly. The walls were made of plaited reeds and bark.

The largest house in each village was the *bohio* where the chief, or *cacique*, lived. Here he would gather with the *mitaynos*, or headmen of the tribe, and discuss the organisation of the community. They planned which fields should be planted and when crops should be reaped. The *cacique* had the final say in all matters affecting the tribe. Each member of the village knew his own jobs. Fishing trips and clearing and planting fields were done by the whole community.

Farming and food

The plants which the Arawaks brought from the mainland and found on the islands were grown in small fields near the villages. *Manioc* was their main crop. The word 'Arawak' means 'eaters of meal', and the meal was the *manioc*. *Yocahu* was the chief Arawak god, the god of *manioc*.

The forests were cleared by burning trees and bushes. The ground was broken with sticks and stone tools and the crops planted. Besides

Arawaks prepare to set out on a voyage. They loaded their canoes with provisions and animals which they needed for settlement.

An Arawak hut, made of a wooden framework of firmly tied posts, covered with reeds and thatch.

manioc, there were also fields of corn, sweet potato, cotton and tobacco. The Arawaks knew how to roll up the dried leaves of the tobacco plant, put fire to it and inhale the smoke.

There were also many wild plants which were valuable to the Arawaks. They knew how to make medicines from the herbs growing in the forests, and used the fruit and bark of many trees for food and household purposes, such as rope-making and basket-work.

In its natural state, *manioc* can be harmful because of its poisonous juice. The Arawaks knew how to extract this juice and keep the rest of the root tuber for food. The women did the planting, and it was also their duty to prepare the food for eating. By grating the *manioc* and squeezing it, the women made a rough grain which they then ground into a fine flour, using a stone mortar and pestle. The grindstone was called a *metate*. The flour was then used to make thin, flat cakes or cassava bread. These were cooked on a flat round griddle made of clay. This griddle was placed on three large stones over a fire and the *manioc* dough was heated into a firm crust.

Two other important root crops grown by the Arawaks were yam and sweet potato. These were planted in fields prepared in the same way as for cassava. The fields were only used for a few growing seasons because, without knowledge of fertilisers to enrich the soil, the earth eventually became unproductive. The Arawaks moved on to clear new plots while they let forest bush take over the old fields. Maize had to be protected from birds, and the Arawaks built platforms in the fields where the children would stand to chase birds away from the grain.

There was hardly any method of storing provisions for any length of time, and so Arawak and later Carib food came almost directly from the fields and into the cooking pot. The cassava bread, however, was made so brittle and dry that it could usually be stored for many months.

In order to have time to do other village work, the Arawaks created a type of stew which was always gently cooking and ready to eat. This was the 'pepperpot'. The main ingredient was cassava juice from which the poison had been carefully extracted. This was put into a large pot over the fire. Added to this were chopped bits of potato, yam, maize and herbs. Pepper was mixed in, as this was a favourite seasoning of both the Arawaks and Caribs.

Besides these cooked foods there was also a variety of fresh fruits—pineapple, star apple, mammee apple, hog plum and pawpaw—growing in the West Indies during the time of the Arawaks.

Fishing and hunting

Although the Arawaks were principally farmers, fishing and hunting were also valuable sources of food. The coral reefs and bays around the islands were teeming with fish, crabs, lobsters and other shellfish which could easily be caught by harpoon or by hand. Further out to

An Arawak smoking tobacco.

An Arawak woman grinding cassava grain into a fine flour.

Fruit eaten by the Arawaks: pineapple, star apple, mamee apple, hog plum, pawpaw and guava.

sea there were dorado, grouper, snapper, jacks, grunt, flying fish and barracuda. At night the Arawaks could easily snare turtles as they came to lay eggs on the sandy beaches. The Caribs did not eat turtle as they believed it made a man stupid!

The Arawaks of Cuba had a very clever method of hunting turtles. They tied a *Remora*, or sucking-fish, to the end of a line and let it swim alongside their canoe. When the fishermen sighted a turtle, they would guide their canoe nearby and play out the line on which the *Remora* was tied. The fish would attach itself to the turtle with the powerful suckers on top of its head. The fishermen could then easily draw near the turtle and lift it into their canoe. In Cuba the Arawaks also made pools on the seashore where they bred and kept fish and turtles to use whenever they wished.

In most of the Caribbean, however, the methods of fishing were much more simple. A bone-tipped harpoon attached to a line was standard gear. Stones with holes and notches cut into them have also been found. These may have been used as sinkers for nets. Hooks of shell and bone were also used.

Fish was usually smoked slowly over the fire on a clay stand, across which sticks were arranged for the fish to smoke on. Meat was also prepared in this way.

Hunting on land was less rewarding, as there were few animals large enough to put in a stew. The iguana, agouti, and Indian coney or *hutia*, gave the most meat. The Arawaks had a breed of barkless dog which they kept as a pet and sometimes ate.

Agouti and *hutia* were chased through the forest into fenced-off enclosures or corrals where they were trapped and caught. Otherwise these animals were clubbed as they ran, or were burned out of their

An agouti.

trees and holes. The large, greenish lizard, the iguana, was often caught while sunning itself on large rocks. Hunters would also imitate the iguana call or whistle gently to confuse the animal and catch it while it remained hypnotised.

Hunters also imitated the cries of birds to lure them into nets and snares. Sticky gum was often hung on a string with some grain, so that when the bird alighted the gum would hold it fast. Catching water birds was also cleverly done; hunters put calabash gourds over their heads and swam slowly towards the resting ducks and waterfowl. Floating gourds were nothing unusual to these birds, and so they were easily taken as the hunters grasped their legs and pulled them under the water.

A *Remora*, or sucking-fish.

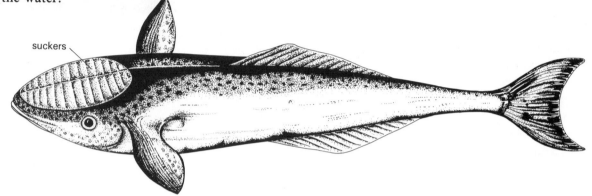

suckers

Village customs

The *cacique* was not merely the ceremonial chief of the tribe. His duties included making and enforcing laws, judging cases, and being chief priest. The position of *cacique* went from father to son, but if he left no heir, his successor would be the eldest son of his eldest sister. Below the *cacique* were the noblemen or captains, called the *mitaynos*.

The *cacique* wore a coat of feathers and strings of beads made from semi-precious stones such as jasper and jade. Bits of gold and copper, called *guanin*, were worn by those of higher rank. Generally the Arawaks wore no clothes, for in the warm Caribbean there was no need. However, as a sign of rank the married women wore strips of cotton cloth hanging from their waists. The wife of the *cacique* wore the longest cotton apron as a sign of her position. The Arawaks painted their bodies with the dye from certain fruits and tree bark. The chief colour was red, but designs were also created in white and black. Colourful parrot feathers were worn in their hair. The Arawaks were very proud of their straight black hair, and wore it in many styles—usually with a fringe coming down to just above their eyebrows.

One of the main duties of an Arawak mother was to flatten the forehead of her infant children. This was done by binding the baby's head between two boards with bands of cotton. It was done very gradually and, because babies have soft skulls, it was not as painful as it sounds. It was thought that a flat forehead was more handsome, created a stronger skull, and made it easier for boys to aim bows up into treetops!

The Arawaks were generally peaceful people, but there were times when different groups would quarrel and fighting would break out. Sometimes plans were made to raid other settlements, and stones, shells and spear handles were prepared for weapons. Towards the end of the Arawak period, the men of each village had to be prepared for war with the Caribs.

The Arawaks had few laws, and crimes were rare. Their only personal possessions were stone axes, tools, and clay pots, so there was no great temptation to steal from one another. If there were any crimes, the *cacique* was the final judge. Theft and greed were most serious crimes, and these offences were punished by being pierced and left to die on a pointed stake.

Worship and beliefs

As chief priest, the *cacique* was responsible for taking care of the sacred images of the tribe, called *zemis*. These were made of clay, cotton, wood or stone, and took the forms of humans, reptiles, and birds. The Arawaks worshipped nature and their ancestors. The *zemi* also represented a supreme being who was the Lord of the land, sea and man. He brought together the three basic elements in the life of the Arawaks, and for this reason he was sometimes called *Yúcahu Bagua Maórocoti*, Lord of the Three Names: Land, Sea and Man (the forefathers).

The Arawaks made *zemis* to make sure that they were always blessed by the spirit. Different *zemis* helped the hunter, farmer or fisherman; others could help to produce children or foretell the fate of raiding parties. The *zemis* had a special place in each hut. Offerings of food were placed on the flat crown on the head of the *zemi* to satisfy the spirit and guard the owner against misfortune. Since the spirit provided them with everything they had, the Arawaks believed that they should always keep the *zemi* well provided with food.

As the *cacique* was also the chief priest, his visions and judgements were believed to be the most accurate. During religious ceremonies the *cacique* smoked large amounts of tobacco and inhaled other herbal drugs to get these messages from the spirits. He would then proclaim to his tribe the meanings of the visions he had seen. What enabled him to do this was, of course, not the spirits themselves but narcotics in the drugs which he inhaled. The Arawaks used 'Y'-shaped pipes to draw fine narcotic powder into their noses. The two ends of the 'Y' were placed in the nostrils, and the other end was put into the powder. In this way the Arawaks drew the snuff into their noses. This snuff was

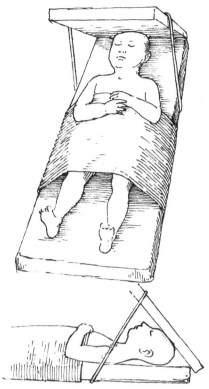

This picture illustrates the method by which the Arawaks flattened their babies' heads.

A Y-shaped pipe, like the ones used by the Arawaks to draw narcotic powder into their nostrils.

63

powdered tobacco leaves called *cahoba*. But to see 'visions' they probably used more powerful narcotics such as *yopo*, made from the roots and leaves of other plants. The Spaniards noted that 'with this powder they would take leave of their senses, becoming like drunken men'.

Feasts and games

Arieto was the Arawak word for both singing and dancing. These were mixed into their religious beliefs and the songs were often about spirits, ancestors, and the life of the village.

On feast days special food was prepared, and cassava beer was shared among the men and women. Dancing took place in the open space before the *cacique's bohio*. On these occasions the *cacique* sat on a ceremonial stool, or *duho*, made of carved wood. The *duho* was usually in the shape of an animal with four stout legs and a head. Sometimes the head had human features, sometimes those of a parrot or turtle. The intricate designs were decorated with coloured beads. coral and hammered metal.

The Arawaks of the Greater Antilles enjoyed playing a ball game similar to that played by the Maya. These ball games were played on large grass courts, remains of which have been found in Cuba, Hispaniola and Puerto Rico. These were probably built by the last group of Indians who came to the Caribbean from Yucatan. Musical instruments of the Arawaks included wooden gongs, drums hollowed from tree trunks, and rattles or 'shack-shacks' made of gourds.

This Arawak ceremonial bowl-stand is two feet high and was found in St. Vincent.

Building canoes

Canoes were often the most valuable property of Arawak tribes. These wooden vessels were the only means of transport between the islands and along the rugged coastlines. Fishing and trading *manioc*, tobacco and cotton would have been impossible without them.

When building a canoe, the men of the village would look among the tall forest trees for one tall and stout enough to build a canoe. They knew which woods were hard and which were soft, which timbers were best for carving and stretching. When they had agreed on a particular tree the men set about felling it. Sometimes they built a fire around the base of the tree and kept the fire going for days until the tree collapsed. Or else they would gather together around the tree with stone axes and chip into the trunk until it fell. The branches were then cleaned off and work on gouging out the canoe began.

Most of the carving, gouging and burning of the canoe was done in the forest where the tree had fallen. For days men worked on the trunk. Women came with supplies of food and drink. Slowly the fallen tree trunk began to look like a canoe. Men chipped into the centre of the log with their sharp stones. Brands of fire were placed in a line

along the trunk to burn into the wood; or else the trunk was placed over a fire in a trench so that a hollow could be burned out. The outside of the hull was also shaped in this way. The canoe was then placed upright and filled with large boulders and water. This caused the sides of the canoe to expand and become broader. This process could take many weeks. At last, when they thought it had been stretched enough, the whole village dragged the canoe to the seashore amidst much singing and drinking.

When the canoe was near the sea, the final touches could be worked on. The wood was made smoother and planked seats were put in. For larger canoes, planks were added to increase the height of the sides. These planks were fastened on by drilling holes and by lashing them in place with fibre rope. The *cacique's* canoe was often painted with bright designs. Paddles were also carved before the canoe was ready for launching. The Arawak canoes seem to have had square bows, while the Caribs developed a pointed bow and stern.

Art and pottery

The Arawaks had no knowledge of metal to make tools and household implements. Their materials were bark, cotton, wood, stone, bone, shell and clay.

They made fine stone tools by chipping and grinding bits of rock. These tools were made by the side of the river or sea. Today, large worn boulders remain to show us where the Arawaks worked at tool-making. Hammocks, or *hamacas*, were made of cotton and bark rope. The cords were knotted into a network, or woven together by the women, to form a rough canvas cloth.

Probably the most outstanding art form of the Arawaks was their

A wooden *zemi*.

An Arawak ceremonial stool, or *duho*, made of carved wood.

65

pottery, and the symbols and designs which were carved and painted on these pots, bowls, incense burners and jars. Most of the islands had clay which was excellent for this purpose. The Arawaks developed the highest standard of ceramics known in these islands. Even on simple bowls and pots the people worked in designs representing animals and spirits. Colouring was made from powdered stone. Bowls were made in the shapes of turtles. Handles were carved to look like heads. Frogs, bats, snakes, manatees, and parrots were some of the animals they symbolised.

For almost one thousand years the Arawaks lived on the low hills of the island coasts in small, peaceful social groups. But another wave of Amerindians was setting off from the Orinoco River region in the south. These travellers were similar in many ways to the Arawaks, but were moving up the chain of the Antilles conquering and subduing each island as they went. These people were the Caribs.

Myths The Arawaks were very close to nature, and their religion and beliefs show this. The stories and myths of the Arawak people are also filled with the mystery of the land, sea and sky. For example, a hummingbird features in a myth about the pitch lake of Trinidad.

There was once a village whose members had destroyed a sacred hummingbird. As a punishment for this deed the whole village sank into the earth, with all the members of the tribe and their belongings. The hole through which they fell became a black mass of pitch where man could no longer live.

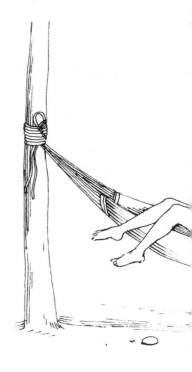

The Pitch Lake myth. The Arawaks believed that this was the site where the Great Spirit destroyed a village where hummingbirds had been killed.

Words to remember

Arawak	*cacique*	zemi
Carib	*mitaynos*	narcotics
ceramics	*metate*	drugs
pre-ceramic	iguana	*duho*
~~guava~~	*guanin*	hammock
	pepperpot	paddle
	Remora	

do and discuss

archaeologists have made studies of Arawak
n your country.

cal library or museum and ask if you may see
Carib artefacts.

nake clay pots in your country? Find out how it

ver eaten cassava?

odel of an Arawak house, using grass and sticks.

e cotton which was grown locally and place it in your
k. Make a drawing of a cotton plant next to it.

ght types of fish which are caught locally. Have you
en fishing?

o you think that the Arawaks respected the land, sea
.y?

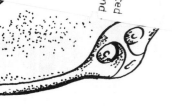

7. The Caribs

The Caribs were one of many Amerindian tribes whose forefathers had wandered into South America. They lived in the tropical jungles south of the Orinoco River in the area we know today as the Guianas. For hundreds of years they roamed through this region and navigated along the rivers and coast, slowly moving northwards.

As they travelled with their families the Caribs raided the settlements of the more peaceful tribes whom they came upon. Often they cleared the forest and grew crops for one or two growing seasons before moving on. The Caribs were also fishermen, but to the weaker and more peaceful tribes of the Guianas, these people were best known as fierce warriors.

In about AD 1000, the Carib tribesmen had reached the river mouth of the Orinoco, and began crossing the sea towards the first of the islands in the chain of the Eastern Caribbean.

The Carib warriors travelled in large canoes and carried with them supplies of food and animals. But mainly they relied on raiding the Arawak island settlements to get their provisions. Carib attacks were swift and fierce, and island by island they conquered the Arawaks.

Let us imagine that we are overlooking an Arawak village during one of these raids. We are standing on the point of a small bay on one of the islands. Below us, huts are clustered near the shore around a small stream of water. Fields of *manioc* and potatoes are being tended by the villagers. If we look across the sea, we can just make out the shape of another island on the horizon. But then we notice something else. Coming towards us over the choppy sea are fifteen, maybe twenty, large canoes. As they come closer we can hear men chanting while they plunge their flat paddles into the water. Quickly they draw nearer and drag their canoes up onto the beach. Before we know what is happening, the Caribs are attacking the settlement from all sides. They are armed with bows and arrows, spears, wooden clubs, stones and brands of fire. The Arawak men are killed and the screaming women are captured. Soon the whole village is in flames.

A Carib raid must have been something like this. After it was over, many of the Caribs settled there and rebuilt the village. They took the Arawak women as their wives. For five hundred years the Carib tribes moved along and settled the Lesser Antilles in this way. By the year 1500, they had reached as far north as Puerto Rico. But by that time people from Europe arrived and the great period of Carib rule ended.

A Carib attack on an Arawak village.

A *carbet*, or Carib dwelling house.

The Caribs were more stockily built than the Arawaks, but basically they were of the same Amerindian race. Like the Arawaks, they were handsome, well-shaped people, graceful, smiling and carefree, with a light-brown complexion and long, straight black hair which they oiled and combed. They wore no clothes, but sometimes tied a strip of cotton fabric around their loins.

There is no doubt that the Carib culture was greatly influenced by the Arawaks. The women played a major part in creating this new Carib culture by passing the Arawak language and social habits onto their children. The sons of these Carib and Arawak parents were expected to speak only Carib, while the daughters spoke Arawak. Other customs were also passed on in this way.

The houses of the Caribs and Arawaks differed only in shape. The Arawaks usually built round houses, while their conquerors made theirs either oblong or oval. A Carib village was made up of a small number of houses, with a *carbet* in the midst of the dwellings. The *carbet*, or big meeting house, was where the men assembled. It was usually 60 to 90 feet long and could hold 120 hammocks. There were many stout posts supporting the roof, and from these posts the hammocks were slung. The roof was thatched with palm fronds or *cachibou* leaves, which were tied down by mahoe cords. Mahoe was the name of the tree from which the cord was made. The *carbet* was entered by means of a small door.

The houses which surrounded the *carbet* were oval in shape and were much smaller. There was only one room, and the walls were made of reeds. The families lived in these huts. They included the father, wives and unmarried children. There were also huts for cooking and storing precious objects such as hammocks, bows and arrows. In the kitchens there were utensils such as pottery and calabashes, known as *couris*. The rest of the furniture consisted of cotton hammocks, small stools and four-legged tables of basket-work called *matoutou*. The materials to make everything which the Caribs used came from the land around them.

A Carib stamp for printing on the body. This design was first made in clay and then dipped in black dye before stamping it over the body to create a repeated pattern.

The chief and the tribe

The Carib chief was the *ouboutou*, who became head man either by right of birth or was chosen for being an outstanding warrior. The rights of Carib men and women were strictly divided. The men gathered around their chief in the *carbet* and made plans for war or for organising the settlement. They usually ate apart from the women and spoke their own language among themselves.

The women's place was to plant, prepare and cook food. They also spun thread, wove hammocks and made the clay vessels for holding food and liquid.

When Carib boys were about fourteen to fifteen years old, they had to take part in initiation rites before joining the men of the tribe. After this the youths were able to take part in the war parties and meetings of the chief. From their earliest years they were trained to be warriors.

Although the Caribs wore no clothes they loved to decorate their bodies. Men and women smeared their whole bodies with *roucou* dye from the *annatto* tree. This bright red dye was mixed with oil and was rubbed on every day. Men also marked themselves with black stains. Sometimes they made marked lines with their fingers or used a clay stamp to print designs all over their bodies.

Caribs pierced their ears and lower lips in order to stick ornaments on themselves. These were bits of stone, bone, feathers and pearls. Around their necks they wore collars of animal teeth and beads. Women wore tight bands of basket-work around their legs. Chiefs and captains wore *caracoli* jewels like the Arawaks, which were shaped like a half-moon. The Caribs flattened the foreheads of their children in the same way as the Arawaks had done.

Some Carib words

nokubu	my body	*kunobu*	rain
nisiru	my nose	*nunu*	moon
baku	my eyes	*kueyu*	sun
niuma	my mouth	*barana*	sea, ocean
watu	fire	*aoli*	dog
tuna	water	*binakha*	to dance

What did they eat?

As with the Arawaks, *manioc* was a very important foodstuff. Women washed and grated *manioc* on small boards covered with sharp, chipped stones. Then the grated *manioc* was squeezed in a long tube of basket-work called a *couleuve*. The juice was put aside for use later and the *manioc* flour was heaped up in wooden containers shaped like canoes. The juice was called *tomali*, and it was mixed into a stew with pimentoes and other vegetables and put on the fire to boil. The *tomali* was the sauce for their food. The Carib families sat around the big pot of stew and dipped their cassava bread into it as they ate.

The women also prepared a type of *manioc* beer called *ouicou* for drinking at feasts. They chewed the cassava, spat it out and let it ferment. This beer made the Caribs quite drunk at their feasts and

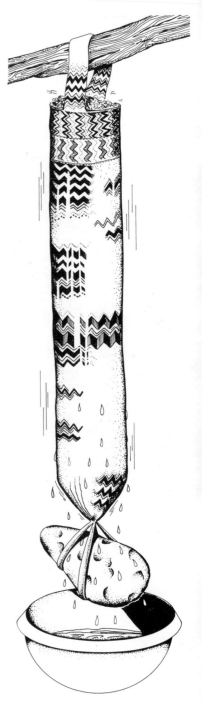

A cassava press for squeezing out juice. This was called a *couleuve*. The weight of the stone forced the juice out of the basket.

often it excited them to fight and prepare for war.

Sweet potatoes and sweet *manioc* were roasted over the fire. Yam and maize were also roasted, but the latter was often pounded into a meal. Peas from wild vines were made into soup.

There were some foods which the Caribs did not eat because they believed that they were bad for their health. Salt, fat and eggs were some of these. Agouti, birds and fish were smoked over fires on a grill made of sticks. This was the only meat the Caribs ate, apart from the pieces of human flesh which they usually ate on feastdays and before going to war.

Clay pottery bowls and jars were used for cooking and holding water and *ouicou*. There were several kinds of earthenware vessels including the *canalli*, *boutalli*, and *rovara*. Carib pottery was very rough. They did not take time to create fancy designs like the Arawaks had done.

Farming and hunting

Besides crops of cassava, yam, sweet potato and maize, the Caribs grew tobacco and cotton which they spun and wove into small strips of cloth. They also made string for fishing and making hammocks. With the islands free for all the tribe, the Caribs planted crops wherever they pleased. Usually they made their farming plots some way from the village. The men burned the trees and bushes and cleared the land, while the women planted the crops and tended them.

The Caribs hunted with bows and arrows, not just to get food but also as sport. For this they used arrows made from slender reeds with tips made of sharp wooden heads. These were different from the arrows used for war.

A Carib shooting fish with a bow and arrow.

Fishing and the sea

Fishing was even more important than hunting and farming to the Caribs. They were always travelling back and forth among the islands, and therefore became excellent seamen. They knew how to use the stars at night to find their way.

The canoes made by the Caribs were of two kinds, and were not very different from those of the Arawaks which were carved from whole tree trunks. The smaller craft, the *couliana*, was at most about twenty feet long and was pointed at both ends. This type was used for fishing close to the shore and could only hold a few people. The bigger boat was called *canoua*, the word we still use today. The largest of these were up to fifty feet long and could carry thirty to forty people. These vessels were dug out of logs and stretched by fire and soaked with water to make the wood expand. It was in these larger canoes that the Caribs went to attack other islands and made long fishing trips.

The canoes were rowed with flat paddles shaped like spades. A long pole was used to guide the craft carefully over reefs. The bark of the mahoe tree was used to tie the large stone anchor. Rafts were also made from the trunks of light forest trees.

Fish were caught in many ways. Using bows and arrows, the Caribs shot fish which came close to the surface, but they also used fishing lines with hooks made of shells. Lobsters were caught in the reefs with harpoons. Conch and other shellfish were easily caught and eaten, while the shells were used to make tools. Many of the islands on which the Caribs lived had streams full of fish. The Caribs knew how to poison the river pools by pounding the leaves of certain plants and mixing them into the water. This would stun the fish, which could then easily be caught by hand.

Beliefs

Carib religion was simple. They worshipped their ancestors and nature and believed in evil spirits, or *maboya*, whom they had to satisfy. The priests, or medicine men, were called *boyez*. Their chief function was to heal the sick with herbs and to call up spirits from the past. Magic charms were used, and generally the *boyez* were little more than sorcerers. They had special huts, where they practised their mysterious rites.

When a Carib died in his own village he was buried in the earth inside his family's hut. The dead body was wrapped in a hammock in a sitting position and was buried with some bowls and weapons which were needed in the after life.

A Carib feast.

War

Earlier in this chapter we learned how a Carib raid was carried out. Much preparation was made for these war voyages to other islands and settlements. When the men of the tribe had decided to raid another island, they held a feast before they set out. Many jars of *ouicou* beer were drunk, and there was much music and dancing. When everyone was very excited, an old woman or often a *boyez* would tell stories of great victories and battles in the past. Pieces of human flesh were shared at these feasts so as to move the warriors to fight more fiercely. This is why the Caribs were called cannibals. They did not eat humans regularly, but mostly on special occasions. Not only did this action make them feel fiercer, but it made the Arawaks, and later the Europeans, fear the Caribs a great deal.

War arrows were prepared. These were different from the hunting arrows in that the heads were made of shell and bone, poisoned with the juice of the manchaneel fruit. Food and weapons were piled into the large canoes and the warriors made themselves look fearful by painting their bodies and putting on all their decorations. Then they took to their canoes and crossed the sea to raid the enemy.

But this life of farming, hunting and war was not to last for ever. Like all the Indian cultures in the Americas, the Carib islands of the Antilles were going to see a great change from the year 1492. By 1650, the Carib people were almost completely driven from the islands and the continent of America. These new people came from Europe, and after them came people from Africa and Asia. All of these civilisations met in the Caribbean to make the lands we know today.

Words to remember

bows	*ouboutou*	*couliana*
arrows	initiation	*canoua*
carbet	*ouicou*	conch
mahoe	cassava	*maboya*
match	yam	*boyez*
matoutou	sweet potato	cannibal

Things to do and discuss

1 Carve a model canoe out of soft wood.

2 The Arawaks and Caribs were similar in many ways, but different in others. Make a list of the differences between them.

3 Draw the Carib weapons you have read about in this chapter.

4 Why do you think the Caribs had so little furniture?

5 What are the advantages and disadvantages of a) a hammock and b) a bed?

6 Draw a map of the Caribbean to show which islands were controlled by the Caribs.

Part Two

People of many different origins live and work together in the Caribbean.

The art of three civilisations: Japan *(below)*, Greece *(right, above)*, and West Africa *(right, below)*.

The Caribbean people are one of the most racially mixed societies of the world. Our forefathers came from each of the four main continents: Africa, Europe, Asia and America. If we walk along the streets of any Caribbean town we see the descendants of every race. The colour of our skins is of every shade: black, yellow, white. In the larger cities we will also find that the people belong to many different religions. In Georgetown and Port-of-Spain, for instance, we will meet many Muslims and Hindus. In other towns we will meet people who belong to many different Christian sects. Because our people have come from all around the world and are now living together in one region, the Caribbean is often called a 'melting pot' of races. This means that West Indians have mixed, and are continuing to mix into one people.

76

This 'mixing' did not happen at once, but over hundreds of years. Not all of the people who came to the Caribbean came because they wanted to come. Some came to escape from being poor in their own countries. Some came just to become rich and then go back home again. Some came to steal and plunder, and many, both black and white, were forced to come here whether they liked it or not.

Today, we are all trying to create a land of peace and unity for ourselves. It is sometimes difficult. We have to create unity among islands and states divided by the ocean and among people of different religions and races. A famous West Indian, Sir Arthur Lewis, once said 'We strive to be ourselves, not Englishmen or Africans or Indians or Chinese, but West Indians'. How do we make ourselves 'one people', out of so many? First we have to understand each other and understand ourselves. That is why we study history.

We read the words 'people', 'civilisation', 'mankind'. What do they mean? For instance, what is a 'Caribbean people'?

Persons who make up one community or nation, or persons who live together in one area, are known as 'a people', or 'the people' of that particular area. A people has its own history, customs and way of life. It may have taken hundreds, sometimes thousands, of years to get together. But eventually a confused group of men became one people. They built towns and villages, planted fields, and made tools. Systems of work and government evolved. There were leaders, officials, scholars, merchants, farmers and craftsmen. They exchanged ideas and wrote poems and stories about the history and the myths of their people. They painted and carved wonderful works of art out of all kinds of materials.

Soon most people got so powerful, wise and wealthy that they went out into new lands to spread their wisdom and power among other groups. When their strength was such that they controlled many different kinds or tribes of people they became an empire.

If an empire lasts long enough, all the people of that empire adopt the customs of the original group who conquered or subdued them. They write one language, live the same life-styles, follow the same customs, and paint and draw in the same way. Such vast groups of people are called civilisations.

We have learnt about the civilisations of America, and the empires of the Maya, the Aztecs, and the Incas. We will now study the civilisations of Africa, Asia and Europe.

What is civilisation?

Often we hear of countries described in terms of civilisation. 'Oh, I have been there!' someone says, 'it is such a civilised country!' Or else we are told, 'The people in that place are very uncivilised'. How can we judge civilisation? All these points must be considered together:

a   the achievements

b   the knowledge and learning

c   the art

d   the beliefs and customs

It is very difficult to say which group of people is more civilised than any other. A big city with many fine buildings may look civilised, but the people of that city may be wicked and violent. On the other hand, a small village in the middle of the jungle may only have huts made of mud bricks and yet the people of that village are kind to each other, work hard, and make beautiful things. Then in another place there may be peace and prosperity, but the people may know nothing about preventing disease or about maintaining good health. So you see how difficult it is to judge civilisation. Let us remember that the spiritual things are just as important as the material things. Civilisation is not judged only by large buildings and expensive life-styles.

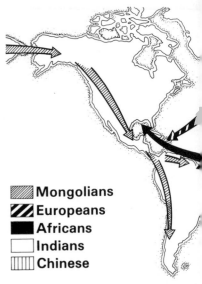

▨ **Mongolians**
▨ **Europeans**
■ **Africans**
☐ **Indians**
▥ **Chinese**

People came from around the world to settle in the Caribbean lands.

This diagram shows the increase of influences and power in groups of men.

Power

In all men there is a desire for control. The story of mankind is the story of man trying to make himself more powerful. The early cave men and hunters wanted power over nature. They wanted power to control the heat and cold, the crops and animals. After thousands of years they succeeded in doing this. Then as men settled into communities, kingdoms and empires, they wanted to control each other.

As we shall see, empires conquered other empires. But none of them lasted for ever. This is why many historians say civilisations occur in cycles. That is, civilisations rise and fall.

Hundreds of years ago our forefathers were part of one or other of the great civilisations. Most of us are of mixed blood; each of us in the Caribbean has forefathers who may have come from different races. They also had different religions and beliefs.

Today the world can be travelled easily. Six hundred years ago, this was not so. One great civilisation knew very little, sometimes nothing, about other civilisations. They were separated by land and sea. Asia, Africa, Europe and America were separated from each other. Let us now find out how these people, who are our forefathers, lived and worked, and where they came from.

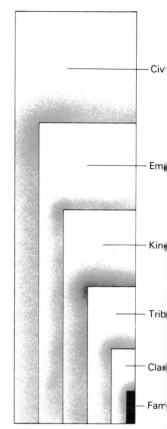

Civ

Em

Kin

Trib

Cla

Fam

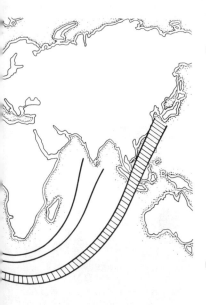

Words to remember

community	mankind	culture
kingdom	ruler	creed
empire	leader	sect
imperial	family	Muslim
tribe	art	Hindu
clan	Christian	forefathers

Things to do and discuss

1 Which of the following do you think are the most civilised things in a society: a good health service, night clubs, democratic government, large buildings, expensive motor cars, schools, a powerful army, farms, libraries, gambling casinos, atomic bombs? Explain what you think is good or bad about each one.

2 Find out the names of four West Indian writers who have published books.

3 Who are the leading artists in your community?

4 How many religious sects are there in your country?

5 Which country does Sir Arthur Lewis come from?

6 What do you think is the difference between a leader, a ruler, and a dictator?

9. Africa

Africa is a continent of amazing variety. This great country lies across a large section of the globe. The great desert of the Sahara in the north gives way to a wide belt of scrub-land and then, in Central Africa, tropical rain forest spreads itself across the river basins of the Niger and the Congo. The vast savannah grassland of East Africa is the home of some of the largest and most beautiful animals on our planet. Even within this tropical region there are mountains so tall that their peaks are covered with snow. In the south there are cool temperate highlands as well as smaller desert areas and bush-land.

Nomadic tribesmen wandering with cattle and camels in Africa today.

The history of all lands is made up of the movement of people from one place to another. Over the past thousands of years many tribes have wandered and settled across the African continent. Some settled and mixed with others or conquered new areas and founded powerful kingdoms. From earliest times hunters and warriors moved with their families across the plains and mountains. Herdsmen with goats and cattle kept searching for new grazing areas and later farmers settled in fertile river valleys to cultivate fields of millet and root crops.

As settlements increased, a system of government and order had to be established. In such places kingdoms and small states developed. Some of these kingdoms were very powerful and grew into great empires. We have heard of the mighty civilisations of ancient Egypt

(above) A Hausa girl

(far left) A herdsman from Mauritania

(left) A girl from Mali

(above) A Yoruba man

(left) A Fulani herdsman

(left) An Ibo girl

(below) A Kanuri woman

which began to expand over five thousand years ago. In later years there were other empires such as Kush, Axum and Zimbabwe or Monomatapa in East Africa and the kingdoms of Ghana, Mali and Songhai on the west coast. Some kingdoms lasted for hundreds of years and then crumbled because of weak rulers, or were overrun by more powerful neighbours.

The people of Africa have always been divided into many scattered tribes, but generally all Africans have originated from four main groups. These are the Arab and Hamite people of the north and along the coast of the Red Sea; the Negro on the west coast; the Bantu of Central and Southern Africa, and the Hottentot and Bushman of South-west Africa.

The kingdoms of West Africa

Most of the people of the Caribbean today are the descendants of Africans who were brought across the Atlantic Ocean from West Africa to work on plantations in the West Indies.

Although West Africa is only one section of the continent, it is still extremely large. Within this area there are many hundreds of tribes, but all of the people are Negroes. The tribes differ greatly from each other and therefore we can only get a general idea of the life and culture of this region. But this will enable us to understand the background of the tribes who came to the West Indies. In all of our islands there are descendants of the Ashanti, Dahomey, Ibo, Mandingo, and other people of West Africa. To simplify our study, let us divide West Africa into two regions. To the north, the kingdoms of Western Sudan which were made up of Ghana, Mali and Songhai. Then moving south we have Central Sudan and the kingdoms along the lower banks of the River Niger and the coast of the Gulf of Guinea.

A map of West Africa, showing tribal areas.

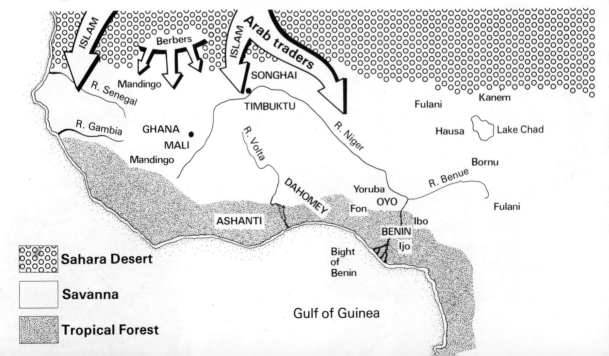

Western Sudan   Ghana was one of the first major kingdoms of this area. Tribes from north Africa settled among the Negroes and eventually there arose the great kingdom of Ghana which got bigger and bigger as more land was won by conquest. The king, or 'Ghana' as he was called, was very powerful. He had an army of 200 000 soldiers armed with bows, arrows and spears.

Ghana became rich from the North African traders who passed back and forth through the kingdom. Gold was in great demand and this precious metal was mined to the south of Ghana. The African tribes who lived in this land needed salt to season and preserve their food. The people from the north brought salt, and traded it for gold. As the large camel caravans passed through Ghana, the king taxed the traders. There was also a trade in slaves.

Ghana was a pagan kingdom. The people worshipped their king as if he were a god. All over the kingdom the chiefs had to be faithful to the Ghana. This system was strict, but it kept the tribes together under peaceful law and order. This attracted many people from North Africa, who settled in Ghana. These settlers were Muslims, or members of the Islamic faith. They followed the teachings of Mohammed and worshipped one god whose name was 'Allah'. They therefore lived apart from the capital city. They built stone houses, mosques and many schools.

After two hundred years of power Ghana became involved in wars with Muslims from the north. The kingdom became divided and organised rule came to an end. One of the gold-producing tribes to the south of Ghana was the Mandingo. These people also began to fight a series of long wars with Ghana. The country was already divided and was soon defeated altogether.

In 1240 the Mandingo attacked and burned the capital of Ghana. Their own capital, Mali, was now the most important city in West Africa. As its power grew, Mali became much larger than Ghana had ever been and it spread south among the Negro tribes and east into the desert. The kings of Mali were Muslims. The most famous was Mansa Musa who ruled from 1307 to 1332. In 1324, Mansa Musa made a famous pilgrimage all the way to Mecca.

After the death of Mansa Musa, Mali continued to prosper for a number of years but then the rulers quarrelled with each other. The government became so weak that parts of the country broke away and became independent.

The next great kingdom to develop was Songhai. For hundreds of years people of that tribe had lived on either side of the Niger River. Soon they rose to become a great kingdom in which all the kings were called 'Askia'.

As in other areas of West Africa, money was then in the form of cowrie shells and gold. The shells could only be collected on the east coast and were therefore valuable. Besides money, a fixed rate of weights and measures helped trade to expand.

Mansa Musa on his horse.

The Friday Mosque at Jenne. Such mosques were built wherever Muslims settled in West Africa.

The wealthy people built large houses surrounded by gardens. They wore clothes made and coloured by skilled craftsmen. Many of the rich were well educated and could write Arabic. The kingdom was divided into provinces ruled by trusted governors and there was a permanent army, mostly on horseback.

In 1590, the Sultan of Morocco sent out an army to conquer Songhai. The kingdom was defeated during a number of wars, and after many years all the old systems and laws crumbled. By the time that the Portuguese adventurers had visited the west coast, the old Songhai lands were ruled by many different Negro rulers.

A camel caravan in the desert.

Central Sudan and the Forest Empires   By the seventh century AD, the area around Lake Chad was populated by Negroes who had settled there after travelling over many hundreds of years from lands in East Africa. Their new land was rich and well watered, and they settled down to a life of farming and cattle rearing.

Not all of the people had to be farmers. Some wove cotton on hand looms and developed ways of making colourful patterns with dyes. Others smelted metal and made tools for the farmers, and weapons for the soldiers. They also produced fine ornaments, masks, and jewellery from gold, bronze and iron. Many carved ivory and wood. Some men were devoted to a life of politics and government.

As the years went by, Berbers from the north mingled with the Negro tribes who lived between Lake Chad and the Gulf of Guinea. These kingdoms never became as wealthy as Ghana, Mali and Songhai. To get extra money they relied on the export of slaves to the kingdoms of West Africa and from the taxation of the people. The main empires of this region were Kanem, Bornu, Fulani, the Hausa states and the coastal kingdoms of Oyo, Benin, Dahomey and Ashanti. Each empire or kingdom has its own history of change and development.

Powerful armies

In most of these kingdoms of the forest and the coast, the army was the basis of all power. The tribes had developed the use of horses in battle. Soldiers on horseback are known as cavalry. The cavalry soldiers were dressed in armour and had colourful spears and shields.

The poorer soldiers fought on foot, armed only with bows and arrows or spears. Most were slaves or peasant farmers, pressed into service by their chiefs. Because these armies were so large it did not matter that many soldiers were not properly trained. Their main task was to capture slaves who could be exported to other parts of Africa. In return the soldiers were allowed to take what they could pillage from the towns and villages which were conquered.

Each kingdom established its own system of government. In Fulani there was peace throughout the country and trade prospered between the Hausa States and across the Sahara. There were good laws and organised taxation. There was a system of civil servants who travelled around checking that the emirs, or district chiefs, were ruling properly. The kingdoms of Benin, Oyo and Ife were not as advanced as some of the other tribes to the north because Arab caravan routes never came into the forest lands. They did, however, have highly organised systems of their own and were famous for the skill of their craftsmen.

The art of the people

Some of the most remarkable treasures of the West African tribes are the bronze heads of Ife. These show the craft of smelting and working bronze in its highest form. Bronze is made from smelting tin and copper together. Over hundreds of years craftsmen had developed the process. They made many other things besides statues and heads of bronze, but to understand the method let us study how a head was cast in this metal.

Most African sculpture is stylised, or symbolic, which means that it does not look exactly like objects in 'real life', but rather it represents or symbolises them. Many of the bronze statues of Ife and other areas, however, were made to look extremely life-like. These works of art were made by the 'lost wax' method.

First a mass of clay, shaped roughly like a human head, is put on a support. This is then covered with wax and the wax is shaped into the features which the artist wants. The wax is allowed to dry hard. The

This cast bronze head is of a queen-mother, or *iyoba*, of West Africa. She is wearing a headdress and collar of coral beads.

whole thing is covered in clay again and left to harden. The wax is
then melted out and the bronze is poured into the space that remains.
When it has set hard, the clay is broken and exposes the finished
bronze head in the same form as that which was shaped in wax. Ornamental bowls and knives, gold and copper articles, and many other
utensils were made in this way.

Besides bronze, gold and copper, iron was also fashioned by black-
smiths who were respected members of their community. Those
metals which the tribes did not mine themselves, they obtained by
trade with other parts of West and Southern Africa. Sculptors carved
wooden statues, masks, and household wares such as stools. Ivory was
another material used by craftsmen. The people of Benin and Yoruba
carved intricate masks and figures from the tusks of elephants and
animal bone.

These diagrams show how a bronze
head was moulded.

The art of making cloth by hand looms is found all over the country. Some tribes usually wore a large loose garment with very long, wide sleeves worn over a simple shirt and pantaloons. Others did not wear much clothing apart from a wrap around the waist. Village artists dyed the garments in bright colours. They used wax, gum and cut-out stencils and wooden stamps to make designs on the cloth. They also tied parts of the cloth very tightly so that it would not absorb the dye and would thereby make a fancy pattern. Leather sandals, bags and belts were made for sale and trading.

Ashanti gold weights used for weighing gold dust.

Religion and worship

As we have seen, the states of Western Sudan and the Hausa and other people of the Lake Chad area had been influenced for centuries by the religion of Islam. But traditional African religions still survived among other tribes of West Africa.

African religion was based on the worship of ancestors and spirits both good and bad. They believed in a Supreme Being who sees all, hears all, and is powerful in every way. Then there were gods for each tribe and family guardians. This may sound confusing to us, but each tribe had a set pattern of worship and ritual which had been handed down from generation to generation.

There were gods of rivers, fruit, war, the home, and for objects which were important in the life of the people. Gifts and sacrifices of food and animals were made to the gods. Just as other religions sing hymns and march in processions, so did the African people perform sacred dances and chants to praise or ask favours of their gods. These had much rhythm, and music was provided by a variety of instruments including drums, string instruments, wooden xylophones, and horns. The music was of many moods—sadness, joy and celebration.

The people believed in the immortal soul. Even after death, the Africans believed that the soul lives on.

Many of the masks and statues were not just carved for beauty. These images were an important part of the tribe's religion. Masks were used by dancers in religious festivals and statues were put in shrines. Each household had its own image or 'fetish', and the family god would dwell in it. This god was blamed or praised for all luck, bad or good. There is also a companion spirit, which guides each man, woman, and child through the day and night.

In each community there was a certain person who was highly respected for his or her knowledge of the spirits. It was believed that these men or women knew how to cure illnesses and could call on the gods to help people with their problems. By knowing which herbs, charms and magic to use they could be very powerful. Members of the tribe would visit them for help and they were important for the dances and rituals performed for the gods.

(left) This beautiful ivory mask was carved by a Benin craftsman about 500 years ago.

(far left) A tribal dance mask used in ceremonies when boys entered manhood.

A shrine in the Palace of the Oba of Benin.

From the chief to the slave

One of the most important systems of West Africa is what is known as the 'extended family'. The 'family' does not only mean close relations. It means grandparents, aunts, uncles, cousins and all the children and wives and husbands of the cousins. Children must have respect for parents, elders and chiefs. Two or three families sometimes make up a whole village. Each member of the family has some special duties to perform.

All land belonged to the tribe and each family shared the work and the harvest. Cattle was owned by families. Chiefs shared power with their families and enabled brothers and cousins to become governors and civil servants.

The chief of each tribe was most powerful. He and his family and court lived in a large compound. The tribes used materials which they found around them to build the palaces. Wooden huts and baked clay walls with thatched roofs were beautiful houses fit for kings. Tax collectors and officers of the army were other powerful people who had large groups of houses, owned slaves and could get services from members of the tribe. Craftsmen were respected for their art and they had to provide the rulers with some of the things they produced. For example, weavers had to provide the court with clothes, and peasant farmers had to give up part of their harvest. This was a form of taxation. This system was in some ways like the feudal system of Europe in the Middle Ages, when lords and barons could get whatever they needed from the people.

In Africa, chiefs could also make people become their slaves. Even the Moslem holy book, the Koran, outlined how slaves should be treated. For hundreds of years men, women, and children had been

(above) A West African family
compound.

right) The carved wooden door of a
Yoruba palace. It shows an official
coming to meet a chief seated on his
throne.

made slaves by being captured in tribal wars or by punishment for crime. They were used as gifts or for trading. There was much slave trading in West Africa between the kingdoms of Western Sudan, spreading south to the forest regions under the Alafins of Oyo and the powerful kings of Ashanti. But a slave in Africa often lived as a member of his master's family. He could work himself free or even marry a relative of his owner. An old Ashanti proverb runs: 'A slave who knows how to serve succeeds to his master's property'.

Traders on the West Coast

The people of the West African kingdoms had not developed as sailors in the way that the Arab traders of the East African coast had done. The fishermen and coastal traders of the Gulf of Guinea generally never travelled far from land. They knew very little about other countries across the sea. However, the great Mansa Musa of Mali recorded a dramatic story of ocean adventure. He said that towards the end of the thirteenth century the king before him had sent two expeditions across the ocean in order to discover what lay on the other side. One fleet of ships was made up of two thousand vessels and another of four hundred. Only one ship ever returned, but some historians believe that these Africans did reach the Americas.

During the fifteenth century the people of Europe became very interested in the world outside their own countries. Merchants sent ships to trade with West African kingdoms along what they called the 'Gold Coast'. In return for Negroes and gold, they gave the Africans guns and other goods from Europe. From that time a great change began to take place in West Africa.

Words to remember

tropical	Hanite	cavalry
rain forest	Negro	slave
bushland	Bantu	sculpture
desert	Muslim	symbolic
temperate	caravan	xylophone
Arab	smelt	Koran

Things to do and discuss

1   What African traditions do you think remain in your community?

2   Give a brief account of the rise and fall of the empire of ancient Ghana. Why did the empire collapse?

3   Find out where Mecca is, and why it is important. Why did Mansa Musa travel all the way across Africa to Mecca?

4   Make a small drum. You can use plastic stretched tightly over an empty tin.

5   Cut out a stencil of an African design from stiff paper. Using oil paint, you can print it on a white 'T' shirt.

6   How was West African religion similar to the religion of the Caribs and Arawaks?

7   Go to the library and find out more about the Muslim faith. Write an essay about it.

(above)
A wooden headrest. Some noblewomen had such fancy hairstyles that they could not lie down without damaging them. They used headrests such as this one. It is a fine example of African wood carving.

The Portuguese trading with Africans off the West Coast.

91

10. India

The people who came from India and China to the Caribbean did not arrive at the same time or in as great numbers as the Africans and Europeans. It was as late as 1840 that the first groups of Asians were transported to the West Indies to work on the sugar estates. These people did not come as slaves but as cheap labourers who were employed in the canefields and sugar factories which developed in the region. The period of bonded labour was usually fixed at five years, after which the Asian labourer was free to return to his home country if he wished. But India and China are very far from the Caribbean and many of them remained here to set up homes for themselves. There are many more people of Asian origin in Trinidad and Guyana than there are in Jamaica and the other territories, because it was the sugar estates in those two colonies which demanded the most labour.

A Hindu temple in Trinidad.

The land and the people

India is a very large country and is the homeland of many types of people. Even today, more than two hundred languages are spoken and there are many different religious groups.

The country, shaped roughly like a triangle, is bordered to the north by the highest range of mountains in the world—the Himalayas. The land to the south is covered with fertile plains and

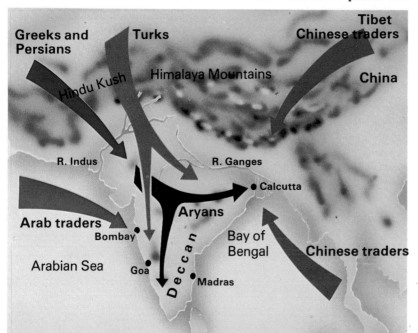

India, showing how invaders entered over the Himalaya Mountains.

The homeland of many peoples

This is an Indian ox-cart. These ox-carts have changed very little from early times.

wide river valleys, such as the Indus and Ganges. From the very early ages of mankind wandering tribes moved through the high passes of the Himalaya mountains onto the rich plains below.

The valley of the Indus river in the north was the home of the world's earliest civilisations. The people of this valley built cities of mud, bricks and cement and had running water flowing into the cities by way of canals and ducts. Walls and canals were constructed to stop the river from flooding their fields and houses. Mohenjo-Daro and Harappa were the chief cities of this valley four thousand years ago. The city buildings stood along fine straight streets; there were swimming baths, shady verandas, and kilns for baking bricks. In these centres lived craftsmen who had learned to shape clay pots and trim them with cleverly coloured figures and designs. They had learned to make sturdy two-wheeled carts in which to carry goods. Wooden boats also sailed up and down the river.

Along the river Indus, the farmers cleared fields and tended crops of barley, wheat, fruit and cotton, using copper-pointed tools.

The Aryans   Some time before 2000 BC the people of the Indus valley were invaded by fierce warriors from the north. These were the Aryans, who came from Western Asia and Persia, seeking fertile lands on which to settle. There was much fighting, and the early people of the Indus were forced to move south, while the Aryans took control of the plains of Hindustan and the banks of the Ganges and Jumna rivers.

93

The Aryans were less advanced than the people they had conquered, but as the years went by their culture developed. The craftsmen worked at many trades.

The Aryans used the language they had brought with them from the west and knew the art of writing. They wrote many books, the most famous being the Veda, the Book of Knowledge. The Rig-Veda is the most ancient collection of religious hymns and stories in India. Their language, religion, customs, laws and the struggles between the various tribes are all recorded in these early books. For centuries the beliefs of the Aryans controlled the people of India. These rules of ritual and worship were laid down in the Veda in a language which was called Sanskrit. The Aryans followed the teachings of this book, which were the guiding principles of the Hindu religion.

Hindus

The Supreme God or all-creator of the Hindus was Brahma, the Creator. He was the supreme ruler, and was perfect. To become like Brahma was the ideal of every Hindu. Holy thoughts were more important than holy deeds, and many people went into the wilderness and lived upon the leaves of trees, sat still and starved their bodies so that they might feed their souls on the thoughts of Brahma, the Wise, the Good, the Merciful. Such men were called Upanishads, or 'those men who sit near'.

Besides Brahma there were other gods and goddesses, each with his or her own strange and colourful life. Two important gods are Siva, the Destroyer, and Vishnu, the Preserver.

The priests of the Hindus were called 'Brahmanis' and made themselves the top of the social class. The divisions in the classes of society were strict. This was the *caste* system, by which each person belonged to a special group or *caste*. The Brahmanis had great power and other people could not share their way of life or even their special language. They were the first of four castes. The second were the princes, noblemen and soldiers; the third were the workmen and craftsmen. Fourth and last were the lowest servants and slaves known as the Pariah, or untouchables, who lived in misery and had to remain forever in the caste into which they were born. They consoled themselves by meditating on the bliss of their future life after death when they could be born again into another caste. We can see that the caste system kept power strongly in the hands of the high castes of priests and noblemen.

Buddha

The rulers of districts in India were called Rajahs. They lived rich lives in large beautiful palaces. One of the Rajahs who ruled a kingdom near the Himalaya mountains in 563 BC had a son called Siddhartha,

Three important Indian gods.
Brahma, the Creator
Siva, the Destroyer
Vishnu, the Preserver

but we know him as Guatma Buddha, which means 'the Enlightened One'.

The prince lived away from all suffering and unpleasantness in the royal palace, awaiting the day when he would succeed his father as King of Kapilavastu. But soon he realised that in the world outside there was suffering and pain, and he realised he could never be content until he had understood the riddle of life. At the age of twenty-nine he left the people he loved and became a holy beggar, or Upanishad. Without a single follower the young prince moved out into the wilderness. He fasted for forty-nine days and nights, sitting on the roots of a tree. On the fiftieth evening he felt a great light come into him and he knew that he had found the truth of life. From then on, Siddhartha was known as the Buddha.

He taught that all our unhappiness is the result of selfishness. We must think of others, Buddha said, speak only the truth, and act simply and nobly to know the peace he called *nirvana*. Many people gave up their way of life and went to tell others about Buddha's way. These missionaries spread Buddhism through China and across much of Asia.

Millions of people follow the teachings of Buddha still, but it has changed a great deal. Now there are many priests and fine ceremonies in Buddhism.

Dynasties and kings

The history of India is long and exciting. Over thousands of years there were many kings, princes,
various ways. Most were warrior
while others inherited their kingd
father to son for several generation
many dynasties in India.

After the Aryans had lived in
years they were invaded, in about
Darius. Years later, Persians too
the Greeks who were sweeping ac
led by a brave young king, Alexa
Alexander the Great.

The Greeks conquered the Pe
army on into the almost unknow
Then down into the valley of th
Indian King Porus waited with ar
in battle array. In 326 BC the In
himself turned back, leaving Gr
states. For the first time the people
people and riches of Asia.

Although the Greeks were goo
men of all races, after a hundred

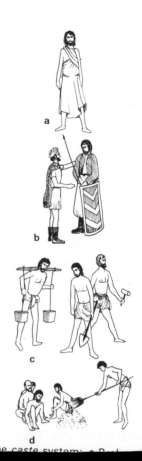

The caste system: a

Then arose one of India's most powerful rulers, Chandragupta. He won back the lands that Alexander had conquered, expanded his kingdom across northern India, and ruled with a firm hand over hundreds of princes and states. He united many of the Indian people.

The work of Chandragupta was continued by his grandson the great Emperor Asoka. He ruled during the third century BC, and unified India into one empire. At first Asoka was a cruel king, but then he became a Buddhist, setting his life according to the teachings of Buddha. He made Buddhism the official religion of his Empire. He travelled through his lands, spreading that peace and love must guide the lives of the people, and that war must end. Great changes took place during his reign. Schools were built, just laws were passed in each state, and art and literature flourished. People carved stories into large rocks, telling the glories of Asoka's Empire. Men studied medicine, and hospitals were built where the sick could be cared for.

But there were still many lords and princes who preferred to live by the sword, and by raiding each other's property. While Asoka ruled these princes remained reasonably calm but, as soon as the great king died, civil war began to sweep the land. The unrest and destruction lasted for hundreds of years.

Order was at last restored by the Gupta Dynasty when, in AD 308, Sumudragupta became very powerful by conquering all the quarrelsome states. The emperors of the Gupta family were wise and just. Like Asoka, they favoured songs, poetry, art and learning.

Mathematics and astronomy, the study of stars, were developed

The Amber Palace, near Nairpur, India.

Visvanatha, a Hindu temple in India.

together as one science. During the Gupta Dynasty men spread the learning of arithmetic, algebra and geometry. The Indians had their own system of numbers and invented the use of 'zero' in counting, and also the decimal point.

It was in the Gupta era that modern medicine developed. It was given the name *Ayurveda* or the 'knowledge of long life'. Besides adding to the studies of the Asoka doctors, they practised general surgery and child care. Indian medicine advanced the theory of good health, or hygiene, and found out what food and drink was best for the body. Indian surgery was quite remarkable considering the metal instruments used by the doctors to operate on their patients. They wrote medical books in the Sanskrit language.

Many fine temples, shrines and palaces were built of stone and adorned with beautiful stone carvings which recalled great deeds of kings and saintly men. Craftsmen worked with copper and bronze, iron, lead and tin, silver and gold. They cast graceful metal images of Buddha and of the Hindu gods. Writers who visited India from other lands marvelled at the laws and learning.

A woman dressed in fine silk clothes.

The Gupta Dynasty lasted for one hundred and fifty years. Then in about AD 500 warriors from the north invaded India, looting the towns and villages. These were the 'Huns'. They almost lived on horseback and roamed through Asia, carrying their tents and possessions with them. They entered India by way of the Khyber Pass and moved in various directions across the land, eventually settling down among groups of Indians.

The Mohammedans

By now we can realise why the people of India are of so many types and speak so many different languages. We find that Greek, Persian, Turkish, Chinese and European customs have all mixed together to form the rich Indian culture. We notice too that between each period of invasion, there was a time when great Indian rulers arose to lead their people. During these times Indian culture developed and there were advances in government, literature, religion and art. Men studied science and built observatories to study the stars. About the year AD 1010 a wise king called Bhoja of Malwa wrote books on astronomy, architecture and poetry.

Selling spices in an Indian market.

One of the most important invasions of India occurred between 1000 and 1100, when army after army of Turkish soldiers attacked the states of India. These Turks had become Muslims, and spread the faith of Islam wherever they went.

The Muslims conquered most of India and made their capital city at Delhi. The Ghuri dynasty of kings ruled the land for three hundred years and spread their power gradually across the whole of India. They did not force the Indians to give up their Hindu and Buddhist religions, but they built mosques everywhere. In Chapter 9 we learnt

of the people in the West African
ng happened in India with the Turkish

the conquerors opened colleges and
oon many Indians became Muslims.
ure adopted some of the styles of build-
vhich the Turks had brought. Together
e centuries, these laid the foundations

d

ions was not India's only connection
ducts of India attracted traders from
from the west, and Chinese and other
he coast of Asia to the ports of Madras
and Calcutta on the Bay of Bengal.

Traders came overland from the Middle East and over the
Himalayas from Tibet and China. They all came to share in the
wealth of cloth, jewels, spices and craftwork produced in the Indian
towns.

The textile or cloth industry is one of the most ancient of India.
Only the Indians were able to create cotton fabrics with a brilliant and
lasting colour. The Indians developed the art of dyeing cloth by the
batik method. For this, wax was poured over the cloth to form
intricate designs and was then soaked in dye. The decorations covered
in wax remained white while the exposed cloth changed colour.
Carpet-making, ceramics, ivory working, woodcarving and glass-
making as well as fine jewellery were some of the other products of
India.

Developments under Asoka's
Empire.

The Muslim invasion of India.

By the twelfth century the less-developed people of far-off Europe
of the East. Not only did they want to
of India, but even more important to
food. For the next two centuries, until
s travelling in camel caravans who
he shores of the Mediterranean and so

r reached Calicut on India's west coast
e across the ocean. In the following
l a trading station a Goa and a new
Eventually the British took control of
ent and only in 1947 did India become
e. At this time East and West Pakistan
vided into Bangladesh and Pakistan.

Words to remember

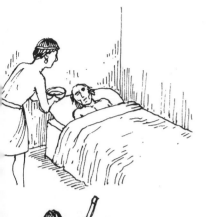

Veda	Buddhist	fabrics
Sanskrit	zero	Turks
Hindu	Aryans	monasteries
caste	Huns	spice
Rajah	Mohammedans	observatory
dynasty	*batik*	algebra

Things to do and discuss

1 Write a paragraph about the Ganges river.

2 What do you think about the teachings of Buddha? Are they similar to the teachings of Jesus Christ?

3 Put a picture of an elephant into your scrapbook. What can elephants be used for?

4 Why did the cruel King Asoka change his ways?

5 Why is zero so important in arithmetic?

6 Make a list of some of the products of India many years ago.

7 Draw an Indian woman dressed in a sari.

11. China

The Chinese people have a recorded history which goes back over five thousand years. Even before that time primitive, black-haired tribes lived along the banks of the Hwang Ho and Yangtze rivers. The yellow soil was rich and the people worked hard. They cleared away marshes and forests to make large fields. They built low, broad buildings of sunbaked earth and they had boats to carry them up and down the rivers with goods to sell, barter and buy. From these humble beginnings there developed one of the world's highest civilisations.

One of the main reasons for the constant growth of ideas in China was that most rulers built upon the achievements of past generations. In some parts of the world, conquering people would sweep away all the achievements of the lands overtaken by them and progress would be made stagnant, but in China this was not so.

China showing the Hwant Ho and Yangtze Rivers. Early Chinese farmers settled along the banks of these rivers.

The ancient land

A Chinese pagoda.

China was ruled by many dynasties, the most outstanding being the Shang, Chou, Ch'in, Han, T'ang, Sung, the Mongol rulers, and the Ming. During the various periods of rule the boundaries of China changed as the armies conquered new lands, or other parts were lost to warring barbarians from the north and west. The Ch'in or Ts'in dynasty gave the country its name, China, for it was during the reign of the Ch'in emperors that much of the land was united under one ruler.

But what stands out even more clearly than the individual style of each dynasty is the overall achievements of the Chinese people—their ways of thinking or 'philosophy' of life, and the great inventions which they gave the world.

The Chinese believed that before action there must be thought. Philosophers and writers declared how life should be run, how peace should be achieved, and how each person could attain individual happiness. The most outstanding of these thinkers and writers was a man called Confucius, or *Con-fu-tze*, who lived from 551 BC to 479 BC.

Confucius.

Confucius

Confucius led a quiet life when China was without a strong central government, and when the people were at the mercy of warrior barons who fought over each other's property.

Confucius loved his people and tried to save them. He taught that to lead a good and useful life you must try to be good to yourself and then be good to others. He did not think that he could change people by making a lot of new laws.

He put together all that was good in the Chinese pattern of life and taught all the pleasant, polite and considerate ways of getting along with others. He showed how these rules should be followed to keep the country strong and happy. He lived during the Chou dynasty, and as a minister of state he tried to influence the Chou lords towards bringing order to the land. A person of real worth, according to the teachings of Confucius, did not allow himself to be ruffled by anger, and suffered whatever fate brought him.

Confucius did not demand that anyone should follow him or worship him, nor did he claim to be inspired by any divine being or god. He was just a very sensible and kindly man, who sometimes went on lonely wanderings to think, or play tunes on his flute.

As a writer, Confucius recorded the good character of the Chinese in religion, morals, customs and political life. China at this time enjoyed one of the greatest eras of culture in the world's history. Another great teacher, called Lao-Tse, lived during the same period as Confucius. But he taught that peace lay in living with nature. A simple country life was the way to wisdom and happiness. Even those people who lived in towns tried to follow his advice by building small but beautiful gardens.

Eight hundred years after Lao-Tse, a famous Chinese poet called Lao Chien wrote a poem which sums up the ideas of this way of life. These followers of nature were called 'Taoists', from the Chinese word *Tao* meaning 'the Way'. Here is Lao Chien's poem:

I build my hut in a zone of human habitation,
Yet near me there sounds no noise of horse or coach.
Would you know that is possible?
A heart that is distant creates a wilderness around it.
I gaze long at the distant summer hills.
The mountain air is fresh at the dusk of day:
The flying birds two by two return.
In these things there lies a deep meaning;
Yet when we would express it, words suddenly fail us.

Years after Confucius and Lao-Tse were dead, religions developed around the teachings of these two men. These beliefs centred around the worship of ancestors and guardians of the home and the land. Outdoor altars and temples were placed in beautiful surroundings, where people made sacrifices to show respect to the mountains and rivers, to the seasons, and to Heaven and the sun.

The first Indian missionaries brought the teachings of Buddha to China in about 200 BC, but it was only about eight hundred years later, between AD 600 and 700, that many Chinese became Buddhists. The peaceful ideas of these three great men of China and India were quite similar and this helped Buddhism to spread over China. Eventually the whole country became Buddhist. There were then far more Buddhists in China than in India itself, the land of Buddha's birth, for many of the Indian people had remained Hindus.

Law and respect

For the whole Empire, law was based on ancient codes or regulations recorded in massive volumes and handed down from generation to generation. The most important laws concerned government and military service. Lack of discipline was severely punished, and there were harsh penalties for taking bribes or failing to do one's duty. Theft, robbery, brawling, and personal attacks were serious crimes. Thieves who stole a second time after being warned had their heads cut off. Mu Wang, who reigned from 1001 to 946 BC, introduced a system of fines for offences instead of capital punishment and mutilation. In all, there were some five hundred basic rules which, if broken, were subject to various forms of punishment.

All land was supposed to be owned by the Emperor. No one had the right to sell land, but of course the Emperors gave the most fertile lands to members of their families or noblemen and wealthy citizens. In this way many peasants were forced to give part of their crops to the lord of the district. Many of them lived almost like slaves, for their work and lives were totally controlled by the barons, who in turn were controlled by the Emperors. While there was much civilisation and learning in China, there were also many people who lived in poverty.

The extensive boundaries of China had to be well defended and, for this, vast armies were raised from among the peasants and led by mighty warlords. Warfare was well developed from an early age and

Mealtime for a Chinese family.

The Great Wall of China near Peking.

excellent metal swords, lances, spears and armour were made. The Huns and other warrior tribes were constantly making raids from the north. In about 200 BC the first Hun Emperor, Shih Huang Ti, built a high wall 1 400 miles along the northern border of the country. Thousands of slaves were put to work on this 'Great Wall', and many died from their labour. But it kept the border safe for four hundred years.

Great inventions

From earliest times the Chinese grew rice in flooded paddy fields and invented water wheels. These wheels had buckets which collected water from a lower level and emptied them at a higher level. Wheels could also turn mills for grinding grain and pressing oil. Wheels could transport carts and turn simple machines.

Wheels could also spin thread. This was important, for the Chinese had found a caterpillar which fed on mulberry leaves and made cocoons of delicate fibres. This was the silk worm. By spinning and weaving the silk fibre, Chinese craftsmen produced fine cloth which they dyed and decorated in many colours. China became very famous for gauzes, crêpes, taffetas, damasks and other forms of silk cloth. Silk trading became one of the biggest businesses in China.

The art of writing began hundreds of years before Confucius. There was a need to remember facts and stories about the land, as well as the laws and customs. Once, in 200 BC, Emperor Shih Huang Ti wanted all the customs of the previous Chou dynasty abolished. All the old books of laws were burned, including those of Confucius. Anyone praising the Chou ways was killed at once. Five hundred scholars died in this way.

The early writers scrawled symbols on wood. If they were writing about a house, naturally it would be too difficult to draw a house every time they mentioned it, so they symbolised it. In Chinese writing each word has its own symbol, so to learn to write you must learn thousands of little pictures.

At first they found strips of bamboo wood were the most convenient material to write on. During the Shang dynasty people wrote on silk paper with brushes dipped in ink. Soon they invented paper as we know it today, which is pulped wood, bleached and pressed into thin sheets.

This picture shows the Chinese rice-paper plant and the method of preparing the paper.

The Chinese were excellent at script writing or 'calligraphy', although instead of pens they usually used brushes. But to write endless documents by hand was a long and tedious task. To make this easier they eventually invented printing. The oldest printed text known was produced in AD 868. Symbols were carved into wood and metal blocks. Ink was spread over the blocks and pressed on paper, so that many copies could be printed in this way. Soon the printing block was replaced by movable symbols or type, set into a frame. No longer did the bookmakers use long rolls of paper as in former times; instead, separate sheets called *pen* were sewn together to form something like this book you are now reading.

Another very famous product of China was beautiful dishes and bowls of porcelain, so fine that today it is called 'china' wherever it is made. This is made from a clay which turns white at the very high temperature of about 1 350°C. Artists painted this with colourful glazes depicting country scenes and Chinese legends. Old Chinese porcelain is priceless and antique collectors judge each piece of china by the dynasty during which it was produced. Thus we hear about 'a Sung bowl' or 'a Ming cup'.

When we talk of cups, some of us may think of tea! And it was the Chinese who introduced this beverage to the world. At first the leaves were pressed and heated and made into powder. This was diluted with hot water to which could be added salt, garlic or orange peel.

One of the most alarming inventions of the Chinese was

Chinese printing.

gunpowder. A mixture may have exploded in the bowl of a Chinese chemist experimenting with various materials. At first, this was used to make colourful fireworks, but it was soon developed as an article of war to be used in catapults, poisoned smokes and flame-throwers. Old books say that, in 1232, Mongols were terrified by a 'thundering machine'. This was probably a cannon cast in iron or bronze.

It is amusing to note that, while gunpowder began as a toy and became a weapon, one military machine later became a toy. This was the kite. In order to send messages to their allies across the battlefield Chinese soldiers made a framework of bamboo, covered it with paper and sent it up into the wind attached to a string. Colourful kites were also used to celebrate feast days.

One very significant example of the use of the wheel was that of the clock, known in China since AD 600. It is quite remarkable that fourteen hundred years ago craftsmen were making chain drives and balance wheels to record the hours of the day. Another invention was the compass. Even before AD 1100 the compass was used on ships to find the north, and so help sailors to plot their course across the sea.

(above) A Chinese wine bowl cast in bronze.

(left) An early Ming blue and white Chinese moon flask.

108

Kites were flown to celebrate feast days.

The Mongols

The Mongols were nomadic tribes of horsemen who dominated the plains of Mongolia to the north of China beyond the Great Wall. They were fierce warriors who struck terror into the hearts of the settled people of Asia. They were excellent bowmen and for over a hundred years swept back and forth across thousands of miles between eastern Europe and the furthest boundaries of east Asia. They found shelter in small round tents. The tents of their rulers, who were called *khans*, were golden in colour and so those who feared them called them the 'Golden Horde'.

The most powerful leader of the Mongols ranks among one of the greatest rulers the world has known. He was Genghis Khan, or 'the Mighty Ruler'. He formed the disorganised warriors into a well-trained and disciplined army of 250 000 soldiers, divided into twenty-five armies of 10 000 men each. With this force he set out to conquer the world. When Genghis Khan died in 1227 he was ruler of an empire far bigger than any there had ever been in the world before.

In 1280 one of his grandsons, called Kublai, conquered China and set up his capital at Peking. He was the first of the *Gen* or Mongol Dynasty and, rather than destroy the great things of China, he encouraged their development. His people so admired the beauty and comfort of civilised life that they soon lost their rough warrior spirit. Some of them took over the religious teachings of Buddhism.

It was during the reign of Kublai Khan that a European explorer, an Italian called Marco Polo, crossed Asia, visited China, and appeared before the imperial court of the great Khan. He marvelled at the progress of China, so much further advanced than Europe. Writing about Kublai, Marco Polo reported that he was 'the most potent man as regards forces, and lands and treasure, that existeth in the world, or hath ever existed from the time of our First Father Adam until this day'.

The overland route to China from Europe was long and difficult. The loaded caravans were slow and expensive but gradually the trading ties between Europe and Asia were strengthened, until eventually, two hundred years later, European sailors found a sea route to the riches of the Orient.

Genghis Khan in later life.

(left) Marco Polo receiving a golden tablet from the Great Khan.

(left below) Marco Polo on his travels.

Words to remember

barter	water wheels	printing
philosophy	silk	porcelain
considerate	cocoon	gunpowder
Tao	bamboo	Mongols
discipline	pulp	Oriental
mutilate	calligraphy	invention

Things to do and discuss

1. Why do you think the early Chinese farmers lived along the river banks?

2. Compare the teachings of Confucius, Buddha, Lao-Tse, Jesus Christ and Mohammed. Are they not similar in many ways?

3. Where do you think is the most peaceful place in your community and why is this so?

4. Why is there confusion when discipline breaks down?

5. Make a list of the great Chinese inventions.

6. Make a letter type of your initials by cutting the shapes out of cork or rubber.

7. Why did the Africans, Indians and Europeans not know about the riches and inventions of China?

8. Stick a picture of a Chinese palace into your scrapbook.

(left) Genghis Khan on horseback in pursuit of the tribes.

12. Europe

While civilisations were growing up in parts of America, Africa and Asia, in many other places people were still continuing their simple, wandering lives. Most of Europe was still a wild and cold land of forests and plains while Buddha and Confucius were teaching in Asia, and the empires of Kush and Egypt were thriving in North Africa.

The people of Europe wandered about, following the seasons, planting a few crops and driving cattle with them as they went. Already some of the men were skilled workers in leather, or toolmakers, or carvers in wood. They lived in rough houses of brush and thatch. They made camps surrounded by walls of sticks and earth to protect them from invaders.

Though they had no written language, their bards and minstrels gathered whole collections of wonderful songs and stories in their heads.

The Greeks

The Greeks were once one of the wandering peoples of Europe. But as they settled down, they built up a civilisation far finer than the one they had captured. It had a high standard of building and architecture, government, and knowledge, as well as a complex set of myths and beliefs composed of several gods.

A Greek ship in a Mediterranean port.

Greece was a land that looked towards the sea. Its ships sailed along the coast of the Mediterranean Sea to trade with other countries. The market places in each Greek town were full of goods from many lands. Like most of the early civilisations, Greece had slaves to do work such as farming and building, as well as rowing the warships and trading vessels.

Greece was made up of many city states, each running its own affairs. The market place was the centre of life of the city government. Greek cities were the first democracies. *Demo* was the Greek word for 'people', so the system was a government by the people. Every citizen, except for the slaves, had a right to vote in the government. Athens, Thebes, Sparta and Corinth were some of these city states.

There were learned men in each state who used their minds to explore new fields of thought. We call them 'philosophers'. 'How is the world arranged?' 'What is wisdom?' 'What is beauty?' Students gathered to discuss such things. Men wrote about the past and the future.

(left) The Parthenon, Athens.

A Greek vase.

113

Artists painted wonderful frescoes on walls. Sculptors carved figures in marble. These statues have been praised by men for centuries. Greeks had a great admiration for personal beauty, and praised the beauty of men and women. Plays were performed in wonderful theatres all over the country and the people enjoyed such sports as athletics and chariot racing.

But life in Greece was not all peace and pleasure. For hundreds of years Greece was involved in wars in the countries bordering the Mediterranean. The most famous leader of Greece, Alexander the Great, spread the empire to distant lands, across Asia Minor and as far as India.

Even among the city states there was war. In the fourth century BC these wars divided the Greek people to the point where their civilisation collapsed.

(left) A Greek philosopher with his students.

(below) A Roman speaks in the Forum.

The Roman Empire

The Roman Empire began from a small city state, just as Greece had done. From about 500 BC the group of people living around Rome fought the Greeks and the Gauls of the north and also the people of North Africa. By the year 190 BC Rome ruled most of the lands around the Mediterranean.

The organisation of this empire was one of the greatest events in the modern story of mankind. In government, many people had a say through the men they chose to represent them. Today countries all over the world, including the Caribbean, have governments based on the model of Rome. The Roman army has served as a model for army organisation ever since. The great Roman code of law is still with us after hundreds of years.

All over the Roman Empire they built villas, towns, forts and aqueducts for carrying water to the cities. Drama, writing, and art flourished.

But there were still other tribes on this continent who had not been conquered by Rome. As the power of Rome weakened, after six hundred years, these tribes overran Europe. Among them were the Goths, the Vandals, and Huns who came from central Asia. For hundreds of years there was destruction, ruin, and fear. These times are known as the Dark Ages. But by the year AD 1000, the long rule of the barbarian wanderers was over.

The Middle Ages

All over Europe the tribes had settled down in towns and villages. The land was made up of many little kingdoms.

Under each king there were lords and barons who ruled firmly over the people in their area. Each lord had a castle and army to protect him and his people from attack. The people were safe, and so they developed as farmers, craftsmen and scholars.

But the castle meant hard work, and in return for protection, the people had to pay the lord by working for him. They had to work in the fields of his private domain, and they had to give him a share of whatever they raised in the little strip fields they worked for themselves. These peasants were called 'serfs'.

(above) Greek soldiers.

A Roman aqueduct. The Romans developed architecture throughout Europe.

It was a hard life. They lived in smoky little one-roomed huts close by the castle walls. The animals lived with them, and only a fire in the centre of the floor kept them warm. Serfs were not allowed to leave the land of their lord. This system was called the 'feudal system'.

A medieval castle with moat and bailey.

Chivalry and the Crusades

To prevent uprisings, the lords developed a system for their protection, out of which came the organisation of Knighthood and Chivalry. Young knights generally had to swear to a code of conduct where they would be of service to their lord, be loyal to duty, and

(right) This painting dates from the Middle Ages. It shows the European king, John I of Portugal, and his court at dinner.

A knight in armour rides out to battle. This was printed from a wooden block and comes from one of the first books ever printed in the English language.

defend the Christian faith. It meant that every man must know his place and not try to rise above his station. So the rich remained rich and the poor remained poor.

The Middle Ages was a time when knights considered it was their duty to go and fight the Turks in the Holy Land. The Turks had taken over Jerusalem and all the holy places which were sacred to the Christian faith. Thousands of soldiers left Europe by way of Venice and Genoa to cross the Mediterranean and fight the 'infidel'. They called these voyages 'Crusades'.

The Church

How did Christianity become the religion of these people of Europe? Ever since the days of the Roman Empire, men had wandered among the tribes of Europe teaching them the Gospel or 'good news' of Jesus

(above) Townspeople building a Gothic Cathedral.

Before the use of printing, books were written and decorated by hand. Here is a page from the Bible.

of Nazareth. He had lived during the time when Rome was in control of the Jews of Israel. He taught about peace and compassion among the people of mankind.

Many of us know the story of Jesus very well. By the Middle Ages, the Christian gospel had spread all over Europe, North Africa and the Middle East. It had even reached parts of Ethiopia and India.

The Christian church was a very powerful force in Europe during the Middle Ages. The head of the church was the Pope who lived in Rome. In every kingdom there were cardinals, bishops, priests, nuns and monks living in monasteries. After some time many bishops became barons. Sometimes the bishops even fought against each other for power.

Artists, builders and weavers of cloth used their talents to glorify God. They built magnificent churches and cathedrals. The church was the centre of learning, the most educated men being priests or clerics. Nothing was done without the approval of the church. Men who studied science, and scholars who asked questions about mankind had to be careful that their teachings did not conflict with those of the church. Otherwise, they would be condemned as heretics and were severely punished. Even the kings and barons had to bow to the power of the Church of Rome.

In the early years of the Middle Ages the church had converted the heathen tribes and had shown them the advantages of a Christian way of life. But as we have seen, gradually the church developed such strength that it controlled even the ideas and thinking of the people of Europe.

Then, all of a sudden, from about AD 1400 something happened which changed many of the old ideas which had controlled Europe for the past one thousand years. Scientists, artists, and scholars brought new knowledge and learning to Europe.

The Renaissance

A monk writing in a scriptorum.

The Renaissance was a time of 'rebirth' for Europe. Scholars looked back at the beauty and learning of the ancient Greeks and Romans. They developed ideas brought by traders returning from distant lands—mathematics from the Arabs and the art of printing from the Chinese.

People were no longer content to sit still while their king and pope told them what to do and think. And so within two hundred years came a burst of expression in art, literature, music, mathematical science, and religion.

Books were being printed. The new invention, the printing press, made books more quickly and cheaply. All the letters of the alphabet were moulded on small blocks of wood or metal. These blocks were put together to form words. The whole tray or 'galley' of blocks was then covered with ink and quickly pressed onto sheets of paper. The first book was printed in Europe in 1456.

With more books appearing, there was a new interest in learning. This is only one reason why, suddenly, between 1400 and 1600, Western Europe moved forward. It was a time when Europeans wanted to find out about everything around them. They wanted to see what was over the next mountain, what was across the sea, and what was in the heavens. The Renaissance was an age of ideas, invention and discovery.

Words to remember

bard	aqueduct	crusade
minstrel	barbarian	gospel
complex	baron	cardinal
democracy	domain	cathedral
citizen	serf	cleric
fresco	feudal	heretic
theatre	uprising	scientist
castle	knight	scholar
code	infidel	The Renaissance

Things to do and discuss

1 The primitive tribes of Europe lived in a very cold climate. How did they shelter and defend themselves?

2 Why can we say that the Greeks were civilised?

3 Greek actors performed their plays with masks. Make a happy mask and a sad mask out of cardboard.

4 Collect pictures of ancient Roman buildings for your scrapbook.

5 Together with other pupils in your class make a cardboard model of a baron's castle.

(below) A printing press in action.

6 How did the church help to educate the people in Europe?

7 How was the feudal system in Europe similar to the systems among the Chiefs of Africa and the landlords of China?

13. Traders & explorer

Very often in history, many important things are happening at the same time. So let us not forget that while the 'rebirth' of learning and new ideas of the Renaissance were taking place, the kings, the church, and the merchants of Europe were still battling away for power and wealth.

The Pope was still supreme head of the Church. However, certain Christians felt that all its greed and power was wrong, and they started new, simpler churches. This breaking away from the Church of Rome was called 'the Reformation'. The new churches were called 'Protestant' churches, because they protested against the established Roman Catholic Church.

Merchants had also become very powerful. They made a lot of money by providing the rich people of Europe with spices, silk cloth, and beautiful carpets and bowls for their homes. These came from the East—from Russia, Arabia, Persia, India and far-off China.

Sailors studying charts in preparation for a long sea voyage.

A time of adventure

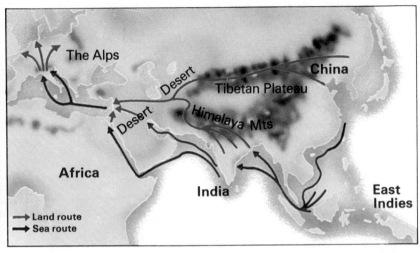

Caravan trade routes from Asia to Europe during the Middle Ages. These journeys made by land and sea were dangerous and very expensive.

In 1245, Marco Polo, an Italian explorer, had left Europe with his father and uncle to travel eastward across Asia to China. After a long and dangerous journey the party reached Cipangu and Cathay, the old European names for Japan and China. There, Marco Polo marvelled at the rich empire and court of the Mongol ruler Kublai Khan. Polo served under the Great Khan and returned to Europe in 1271, where he wrote a book of his travels.

The richest merchants in those days were the Italians. During the Crusades the ship owners had taken Christian soldiers to fight in the Holy Land. By the time the Crusades were over these sailors had developed a lively trade in goods between Italy and the Middle East.

Some ships went past Constantinople to the eastern ports of the Black Sea. But many docked at Mediterranean ports like Acre and Tripoli. They unloaded their cargoes of wool and grain from Europe and reloaded with spices and perfumes, carpets and silks from eastern caravans. Back in Italy most of the goods would go out on caravans again over the Alps to markets in Germany and France.

Then the Turks and Arabs took control of the overland trading routes to the East and Africa. It became difficult for the Europeans to get the goods and spices they so desperately wanted. The western traders realised that they would have to leave the Mediterranean and try to find a route to the Indies by the way of the Atlantic Ocean.

Perhaps by sailing down around Africa, they thought, they could reach the East Indies and Cipangu. But the Atlantic could be wild and mysterious, and there were strange tales about the monsters and whirlpools which lay over the horizon. Most people still believed that the earth was flat and that by sailing too far ships would fall off into nothingness.

Ships and sailors

The Roman ship was only a large open boat with a beaked 'prow' and one square sail. The oars were manned by slaves. At the time of the Crusades a deck was added, a few more sails, and little 'Castles' at the 'stern' and 'bow'.

When the ships began to explore into the Atlantic, the sailors developed larger, stronger ships. More masts and sails were added, and three decks as well as larger holds for cargo were built.

The big, square sail in the middle was called the *mainsail*, and there was a little one above called the *topsail*. The *foremast* had its *foresail* and also a small topsail. The *mizzen* mast in the stern had a triangular sloping sail called a *lanteen*. These larger ships were called *caravels*. All ships carried cannons and guns to defend themselves.

An astrolabe. The astrolabe is an instrument for measuring the altitude of heavenly bodies, from which latitude can be calculated.

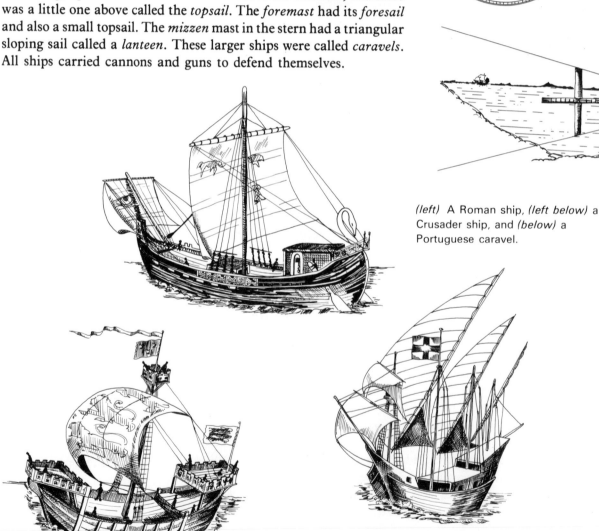

(left) A Roman ship, (left below) a Crusader ship, and (below) a Portuguese caravel.

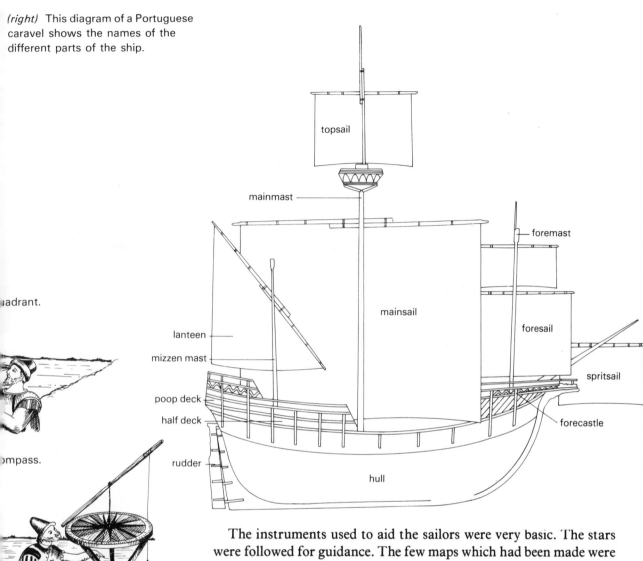

(right) This diagram of a Portuguese caravel shows the names of the different parts of the ship.

topsail

mainmast

foremast

mainsail

lanteen

foresail

mizzen mast

spritsail

poop deck

half deck

forecastle

rudder

hull

ıadrant.

ompass.

The instruments used to aid the sailors were very basic. The stars were followed for guidance. The few maps which had been made were very bad and often incorrect. Since the middle of the thirteenth century the Europeans had used a simple compass with a magnetic pointer to find the north. This had come to Europe from China by way of Arabia and the Crusades. With it, they were able to determine their position when out of sight of land. The quadrant and astrolabe were other instruments used for this purpose. By lining either of these instruments up with a certain star each night and checking the degree marks on the instrument, the sailors could calculate how far they had travelled each day. They also used the sun at midday for this purpose. With the compass to tell them in which direction they were going, and the quadrant and the astrolabe to determine the distance, they could follow the course of their ships on a map.

Life for the ordinary seaman was very hard, and it continued to be so for hundreds of years. Criminals and common thieves were the type of men who most often manned these ships and often men in seaports were forced or 'pressed' into joining the crew.

In their quarters the sailors barely had room to lie down on the hard boards, and they had very poor food. They lived on biscuits, cheese, salted meat and salted fish which soon rotted in the heat. Water was kept in small wooden barrels and easily became slimy and brackish. As they had no fresh vegetables when at sea, sailors often suffered from a skin disease called scurvy. Captains had to be very brave and powerful, sometimes even brutal, to command ships under these conditions.

Portugal leads the way

The merchants of Europe had developed new methods of trading. No longer did they simply exchange a woollen blanket for a bag of spices. They demanded payment in gold and silver. They established banks and dealt in 'currency'.

Now the lords wanted lands where they could get this gold. Europe already knew about the rich ports of Cathay and Cipangu. People had heard also from Arab traders that down the coast of Africa there was the land of Guinea where gold was to be had in large quantities. Because she had a very clever prince, Portugal was already leading the race for gold.

Prince Henry of Portugal was responsible for many improvements on sailing ships. He encouraged sailors to use the most up-to-date equipment and ships. He felt that those who were in charge of ships should know enough about science and geography to be able to develop Portugal's system of shipping. Because of this he was known as 'Henry the Navigator'.

Encouraged by Prince Henry, and having studied geography and astronomy to help them navigate, the Portuguese sailors began to sail down the West Coast of Africa. With each voyage they went further down the coast, and by 1472 they had sailed as far as the Bight of Benin. They brought back news of wealthy African kingdoms which were willing to trade in slaves and merchandise.

In 1484 the successor of Prince Henry, King John II, set up a special committee to deal with matters of navigation and routes to the East. The scholars on this committee studied a confused mass of books and papers on geography. These included the work of the ancient Greek geographer Ptolemy, Marco Polo, and other thinkers and travellers through the ages.

In 1487, Bartholomew Diaz was sent with three small ships to find a way around Africa. He sailed further than any European had done before. After being blown out to sea by a storm, he found that his ships had sailed round the south of Africa. Diaz had found the dream of Henry the Navigator—the sea route to the Indies. Five years later an even more amazing voyage occurred. And this time it was not Portuguese ships which led the way, but three Spanish vessels captained by an Italian called Christopher Columbus!

Portuguese caravels.

Prince Henry of Portugal, as 'Henry the Navigator'.

The Portuguese explorers.

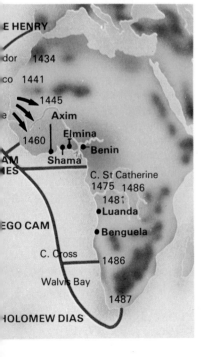

E HENRY
dor 1434
co 1441
1445
e Axim
1460 Elmina
Benin
AM Shama
ES
C. St Catherine
1475 1486
1481
Luanda
EGO CAM
Benguela
C. Cross
1486
Walvis Bay
1487
HOLOMEW DIAS

Words to remember

The Reformation	bow	compass
Protestant	prow	astrolabe
Catholic	stern	quadrant
Cipangu	scurvy	chart
cargo	currency	map
whirlpool	equipment	merchandise
oar	navigate	geography

Things to do and discuss

1   How did Marco Polo get to China?

2   The Italian seaports of Venice and Genoa were full of rich merchants. How did they become wealthy?

3   Fill three pages of your scrapbook with pictures of ships through the ages, from early times to the present day.

4   Why were sailors frightened of crossing the Atlantic Ocean?

5   Make a map of your school playing field. Imagine you are a ship on the ocean and using a compass. Chart your way from north to south across the playing field.

6   Trading schooners used in the Caribbean today are about the same size as the largest Portuguese caravel. Try to visit one of these schooners to study the masts, rigging and sails.

Index

Acknowledgements

The author and publishers are grateful to the following for permission
to use photographs and illustrations in this book:

ZEFA Picture Library (UK) Ltd: pages 12, 37 (top right), 80 (bottom
    middle and top right), 89 (top), 105

T H O'Sullivan: page 16 (top)

Picturepoint Ltd: page 17 (bottom)

Barnaby's Picture Library: pages 25, 40, 93, 96 (both)

Peabody Museum of Archaeology and Ethnology: page 28, cover
    (back bottom)
The Trustees of the British Museum: pages 13 (top), 16 (bottom left
    and right), 29, 32 (bottom left and right), 65 (top and
    bottom), 76 (bottom right), 77 (top and bottom), 85, 88 (top
    left and middle), 89 (bottom), 90 (top), 108 (top), 113 (right),
    cover (back top)

Biblioteca Nazionale Centrale, Florence: page 33 (right)

The Mansell Collection: pages 34 (bottom), 110 (all), 111 (bottom)

The American Museum of Natural History: page 36 (top)

Österreichische Nationalbibliothek, Vienna: page 37 (bottom right)

Museum für Volkerkunde, Vienna: page 37 (top left), cover (front)

Robert Harding Associates: page 44 (top left)

Keystone Press Agency: pages 45, 54

Mary Evans Picture Library: page 46 (bottom)

Anne Bolt: pages 49, 51, 92 (top)

Bruce Coleman Ltd: pages 53, 61 (top)

Craig Burleigh: page 76 (top left)

Colorific Photo Library Ltd: pages 80 (bottom left), 84, 97 (both), 113 (left)

Alan Hutchison: pages 80 (bottom right), 81 (all)

Paul Popper: 88 (right)

Museo Naval, Madrid: pages 124 and 125 (top)

The Daily Telegraph Colour Library: page 101

Sotheby Parke Bernet & Co: page 108 (bottom)

Elisabeth Photo Library: page 115

Reproduced by permission of the British Library Board: pages 116 (bottom), 117 (left and right bottom) Cotton MS Nero D.IV. f. 27 and Royal MS 14. E. IV. f. 244v

The author and publishers acknowledge the assistance of the following in providing reference for line and colour illustrations:
Aldus Books Limited: page 124 (bottom)

The British Library: page 44 (bottom)

The British Museum: page 95 (bottom)

The Mansell Collection: pages 9, 43 (top), 94, 102, 106, 107, 111 (top), 114 (all), 116 (top), 117 (top), 118 (middle and bottom), 122 (bottom left and top right), 123 (all)

Mary Evans Picture Library: page 42 (top)

Peabody Museum of Archaeology and Ethnology: page 31 (bottom)

Radio Times Hulton Picture Library: page 122 (bottom right)